# Impr

# your self-

# esteem

## A Proven Program of

## Cognitive Techniques.

Please note that the information in this document is for educational and entertainment purposes only. All information must be accurate, up-to-date, reliable, and complete. No warranty is given or implied. The reader confirms that the writer does not need to provide legal, financial, medical, or professional advice. The contents of this book come from many sources. Contact a licensed expert before trying out the techniques described in this book.

**Table of content**

## Introduction

Confidence is essential in the world. Your faith determines the way you live. Specify how you interact. Determine the value you ascribe to yourself and how you feel. When he lacks confidence, he cannot trust himself. You don't trust yourself to be trustworthy. You don't trust yourself to be worth anything. You cannot see how capable you are, and it's dangerous. Self-confidence does not have to look for someone who thinks is best, brave, and bold. He is a person who trusts himself.

He is a person who has sufficient confidence to ask for what is needed, to take risks, and to believe that it has value. This person can respect himself and can be very helpful in maintaining a healthy and happy life.

Self-confidence develops in early childhood and is extremely easy to break or break if you don't have the support system you need in those early days. Even if your self-esteem has collapsed, be it because of education, abuse, or for any other reason, you do not have to live with this dissatisfaction within yourself. You can learn to be confident, and in doing so, you will stop doubting yourself. You can develop the confidence you need to succeed. You can check your doubts and make sure you can live for yourself. This book is here to help you get there. Although there is no easy solution that will make you stop doubting yourself, you can learn to be confident enough and resistant to recovery as soon as you discover that something happened or went south. You can be sure that you will do your best.

On these pages, you will find that self-confidence should not be impossible for you. You can learn to develop it, and this book will guide you along the way. You will learn about confidence. You will learn how self-confidence and self-esteem are not the same. You will learn to recognize signs of faith, and if you see these signs, you will learn how to start developing confidence. Several exercises will be provided to help you eliminate some of the worst self-confidence from life and how to begin developing this self-esteem from scratch.

Remember that sometimes everyone suffers from doubt. This is normal and expected. You are only human, and people sometimes doubt themselves. Okay, but it's unfair when this doubt and lack of confidence begin to wreak havoc on your life, causing measurable damage that could be avoided if it were a bit more assertive.

Self-esteem is one of those things you feel everywhere. If you connect to the Internet to see self-improvement, you will probably find yourself flooded with headline articles such as "How do you get high self-esteem?" "What happens when you have low self-esteem?" and other similar titles. However, self-assessment is not as simple as a fashion problem, which should only be taken into account when scrolling through social networks and finding the fashion object that advertises it. This is much more important and deserves full attention.

When your self-esteem is terrible, there are many other problems. Your self-esteem controls what you feel for yourself, and if you feel unwell, you are probably not particularly functional. If you think that you are not a right or talented person, you may have difficulties in various aspects of your life. The life of someone with self-esteem is full of uncertainty, complicated relationships, and failures. For this reason alone, you must strive to outdo yourself once and for all. You don't have to live your life suffering, still feeling like you're not the right person. You can learn to develop your self-esteem to make sure that you love the skin you are in.

The following chapters will guide you through the learning process to do so. You will receive self-esteem that will let you see what it means to have low self-esteem. Information will be provided on the relationship between social anxiety and self-esteem. You will learn to recognize if you have low self-esteem. Before continuing with the book, you will receive a grade that will help you understand the conditions for self-assessment. From there, you'll learn how to develop self-esteem. You will learn how to put an end to self-destructive thoughts. You will learn to recognize your actual value. You will learn to create unconditional love for yourself. You will learn to have compassion for yourself. Finally, you will learn to overcome social anxiety.

There are many books on the market on this topic, thank you again for choosing this! Every effort has been made to contain as much useful information as possible. Have fun!

# Chapter 1: What is confidence?

When you look in the mirror, do you like what you see? Do you see someone who is safe and capable or someone who disappoints you? You don't have to answer aloud and even tell someone how you feel if you don't want to but think for a moment. Depending on your answer, you may be able to recognize your self-esteem in a relatively simple way. If you like who you are and see someone you can trust, you probably have a relatively high level of trust in him, but if you feel ashamed or ashamed when you look at yourself, you may have problems that should be solved if you ever expect existence and proper functioning healthy and productive.

You need to interact with people. You must feel that he is credible or capable of making the right decisions for you. This chapter tries to show how vital your self-assessment is so that you can recognize the importance of working at self-assessment levels. You can't say enough: your self-esteem will affect your whole life.

Confidence

Just relying on yourself is your approach to yourself. It's a summary of how you perceive your skills and whether you can do things that you can. You can trust yourself and judgment: you think you can make good decisions that are right for your particular situation. Think about everything that would happen.

When you trust yourself, you agree to be worthy. Remember that skill is not perfection; In fact, it's incredibly likely that everything you do can always be improved because there is still room for improvement in life. However, you should be able to recognize that there is always room for improvement, and that is fine. You can trust yourself that you are competent but not perfect. You know where you are trained and what areas need improvement. You can see the difference and try to improve everything you fight, simply because you have the confidence to remind yourself that you are capable and you don't just have to end up defeating or fighting, as everyone can

Self-confidence makes you see yourself in a positive way and you can recognize who you are. This means that you feel it's worth it, and you can accept who you are. You don't have to be perfect for yourself and still feel comfortable with your skin.

Self-confidence can come and go. It may be present in some areas and missing in others. There is no one way to deal with confidence, and if you find that you lack confidence in various areas of your life, such as a lack of confidence in finances or relationships, you can spend some time focusing on these matters. Remember that even if faith is something that says you can accept yourself for who you are, you should never feel that they should allow low confidence for who you are. You can always improve, and you have to do it for your good.

The importance of self-confidence

This confidence is crucial in several aspects of your life. Define your relationship. Define your perception of yourself. Determine how you interact with others and be successful in everything you do. Determine how you take care of yourself and more. If you think that your self-esteem will expand and touch all aspects of your life, it will be easy to accept that it is so essential to develop and maintain it.

For a moment, think about someone who sees a picture of a lack of confidence; You probably think of someone upset, ashamed, and afraid to say what you think. Perhaps you have scared continuously or stressed your body language or showed signs of discomfort in virtually all contexts. She doesn't do a particularly good job at work because she is always too busy questioning herself and her skills. He fights at home because he is afraid to make decisions or tell his partner what he needs, for fear of being judged or not knowing what he needs. She doesn't easily make friends, because the people around her usually don't respond well to who she is, just because she has difficulty presenting herself in a meaningful or credible way. She still seems insecure because she is not confident.

Now consider someone you trust. He probably has a high head and shows that she is confident. You can tell others what you think because the opinions of others do not determine it. Instead of seeing others define their value, they live by the motto of wanting to be happy and doing what they want instead of focusing on what others want. Her self-confidence means that it is ready to concentrate wearing and care about each other, instead of worrying how others see it.

Does this mean that a woman with a large f above certainly you never in doubt you, is it always safe? Not at all: it is likely desired that you are in a situation how to make it regularly, but since f is can also rely on yourself and your abilities choice to recognize the correct course of action, you are willing to follow what you said. Able to understand what is right and what is terrible, and is ready to take a chance.

In case something goes wrong and it's always about "when" and not "yes," those who have confidence in themselves will be much better prepared to deal with the situation. You can count on the fact that you will make the right decision, and you will not be paralyzed by doubts that may convince you that you cannot make the right decision in this matter. You will learn exactly what you need. This is key: it can better manage conflict.

Self-confidence matters not only in personal problems. This can be seen in body language. This can be seen in the tone and manner of service. He is continually spreading his level of confidence to everyone around him so that everyone can see it, and others understand it. People who think they don't trust themselves trust you less often; After all, if you don't even trust yourself, why would anyone worry about trusting you?

## The real strength of confidence

Let me give you a hint of secrecy. It's a secret because many people don't like to admit it. The secret is that many people are not sure; Many people lack confidence. Don't be too excited. Lack of trust does not necessarily mean that they do not have absolute certainty. They lack confidence. In other words, it is below the level they need to live a full life. Now, this revelation is quite apparent. You look at the whole experience of people you know, and I can guarantee that 80% of life will be below their maximum potential. In other words, they are capable of much more, but they are happy with an experience that is several levels below this potential. They settle down; They take second place. They don't go as far as they can, out of life. Again, the reason is a lack of trust. They don't have enough confidence. That's why people who trust themselves at high levels are very magnetic. People who do not believe are attracted to safe people. Don't be too excited. It is easy to see the positive side of it; It's straightforward to see people who invite and encourage you.

The most important thing, whether they say it or not, is that I am drawn to you because you have something that I do not have at a high enough level. However, it may incorrectly attract people. Some people lack trust and know it, so they try to attack, reveal, or deploy people who have more confidence than they do. There is always such a change. The most important thing is that in every form, safe people are "magnetic" precisely because they make people around them feel comfortable. There is again negative magnetism because people who envy you what you have. They want to feel comfortable, but they feel they must attack you because they think it's the only way to compensate for the lack of confidence. However, when you trust, you are automatically magnetic. Confident people meet other people's perceptions or want comfort and support.

In other words, people around him are looking for leadership. They are like lost sheep looking for a shepherd. I know this sounds offensive because when you tell someone who's acting like a sheep, don't be surprised if you get a blow to the mouth. But that's the truth, people on one level or another don't have enough confidence and know it. That is why they naturally attract people with a clearly visible and easily detectable level of confidence. Why did this happen? Why are people looking for leadership? Well, some people make people around them feel that things are possible. This is a sign of leadership. When you make people around you think that certain things are possible, they may not have enough of them.

Why? Left alone or left alone, they feel things are harder than they are. They think that this is not easy and that there are many obstacles along the way. When you come to inspire and feel that things are possible, you can't avoid sitting and paying attention. You make them feel something that generally can't feel lonely. If you are confident enough, they will make others think that things are not only possible but also likely. That is what people are looking for in leadership. That's what people are looking for in their social circles. Have you ever noticed groups of teenagers and some of them are more aggressive than others? Well, when you take a group of teenagers who are otherwise shy and add a leader of the same age who motivates them to do certain things, you'll be surprised at what this group can do.

Of course, this can develop positively or negatively.

Most of the criminal and group violence heard in the news generally involves groups of teenagers who have one or two leaders who encourage them to feel that certain things are not only possible but also likely. Stealing a liquor store? Well, if the leader is not in the mix, it is merely an inactive fantasy. When the right person appears among them, it's only a matter of time before the group breaks down the liquor store.


Bottom line

Confident people can create a "field of personal reality" around them. It is easy to walk and think that some things are possible and some are not possible. Everyone has the right to do so. However, when you meet someone very confident, it is straightforward to fall under his influence. It is effortless to believe that they are convincing. Now your answers to the questions you may face may not be better than the answers, but they would not look that way. Why? His level of self-esteem is so contagious that he convinces you to think that if that person seems so enthusiastic about what he is saying, it must be true. It can be entirely correct in its conclusions because it believes that it can be based on logic, understanding, and experience, but everything that comes out of the window. This person's trust leaves you without a word and allows this factor to convince you to draw the opposite conclusion. Confident people also create a personal reality around them through group cohesion. Believe it or not, when two or more people gather in the same group and begin to repeat certain things, they start to hypnotize. They are beginning to think that the ideas they have a problem with are real. There is something that the group believes, and the reason for the group's coherence is, they thought, confident people. When this happens, certain people can gather individual strengths and group skills to achieve common goals. This is the essence of leadership. It's important to understand that just because you can do it because of your natural trust does not automatically mean that you will have formal leadership roles, at least at the beginning. In other words, just because you can do it, don't think your boss will automatically say, "Okay, he's been promoted." Sometimes it takes some time; there is an office policy after all. However, the place where you work would be stupid if you neglect your organic leadership because if people have sophisticated titles or occupy high positions in the hierarchical table, their natural leadership is not undeniable. It's a waste of an organization that still turns a blind eye to the organic direction of some people in the organization. I have to remember that because it's easy to think of confidence as something "nice to have." No, this is not an option. If you want to go anywhere in your life, if you're going to reach your full potential, if you're going to stop living frustration and disappointment, you need to invest time, effort and energy to develop your self-esteem and become an organic leader who will sooner or later become a formal leadership role.

## Chapter 2: What is self-esteem?

Stand in front of the mirror for a moment and look at yourself. Just look at yourself and think about how you see yourself. What do you feel about yourself Do you think you are healthy and capable? Do you seem like a waste of space? Do you feel happy or disappointed? Bad or comfortable and open? What you think about yourself is ultimately a direct reflection of your self-esteem. Your self-esteem is the respect you have for yourself, and it's a way of thinking about yourself. It's the way you trust yourself and how much you think you can.

Ultimately, self-esteem is essential if you want to be successful, and self-esteem is not enough, you must have the right level of self-esteem If you do not have sufficient self-esteem, you will find yourself feeling defeated or generally unable, which prevents you from taking risks that would otherwise be of great benefit to you.

It is important to remember that your self-esteem can always change. How you feel one day may not necessarily be how you think the next day. However, this is often entirely consistent. If you often believe something for yourself, you can be sure that this is your true self-esteem. If it turns out that self-esteem is not balanced, or if you think that self-esteem has caused problems, you should somehow calibrate it again. This is where the book appears.


## Self-esteem

Self-esteem is more than the slogan used in articles to get opinions on the Internet. This is an essential psychological concept that must be understood to know what a person thinks about himself. Self-assessment describes self-esteem; rather, how much you appreciate or respect yourself. If you can see yourself and say with certainty that you generally like who you are, and you can confidently and honestly say that you want the skin you are in, you will probably have healthy self-esteem. However, if you feel that you are unable, stupid, unable to do something right, and even hate yourself, you may suffer from low self-esteem.

Your self-esteem is a personality trait. This means that this is mostly part of who you are as an individual and, for the most part, will remain relatively constant. You will have similar opinions about who you are and what is worth most of your life unless something extraordinary happens. This means that you can generally assume that your self-esteem will not change unless you work on it. Of course, it will go down to a certain level if you do not have the skills to fix it.

Self-esteem usually comes from many other places. It's not just a thing in itself, and it's a conglomerate of different thoughts and beliefs about who you are. You can consider your appearance, intelligence, relationships, or habits. You might think about how you react to others or why you do what you do. Everything is related to your self-esteem. You may have the impression that your appearance means that they will laugh hard you finding protracted period partner, yellow rice Tray with the channel can feel desired that you're not doing anything good, which means that you are not worth much.

In particular, his life strongly influenced by him. Her personality is part of her: some people who are concerned may suffer from low self-esteem more often than those who have higher self-esteem. Their life experiences, especially in early childhood, are another critical determining factor. If you grew up with a supportive family, surrounded by people who helped you feed this self-esteem, chances are you'll feel much more comfortable.

However, if your family criticizes everything you do, you will probably feel less confident. If you've met with a lot of criticism or too negative people, you hear more often than you don't deserve it. As a result, the voice that speaks to you becomes the voice that you talk to yourself. If your parents were nice and helpful, you'll be much more sympathetic to your mistakes. You will find that this is not the end of the world. However, if someone shouted at you or said that you rarely do things the right way, you are much more likely to tell them later. It only shows how vital the voices used by children can be when considering the overall development of children as they grow up.

The importance of self-esteem


Because self-esteem is the way you look at
yourself, it is crucial. It's more than just these
thoughts: all these thoughts also imply. Your
thoughts will have a direct impact on your
behavior and the way you choose to interact
with other people. If you think you are
incapable or that you often describe yourself
as an awkward idiot, you probably won't take
any risk when you find someone you find
attractive, instead of going out and risk trying
to talk to the other person, instead decide
what you will do to avoid them. At all costs,
because you know they would never want
someone as stupid as you. His self-esteem

effectively prevents him from succeeding, convincing him that trying to achieve this success has no value because he will never make it. You cannot manage when you are a fool, incompetent, ugly, evil, shy, or whatever your mind thinks, and you believe with all your heart. The beliefs you have, these negative opinions about you, hold you back. The truth is that even If you are ugly, stupid or desired usable, as  you think still deserve the same human decency, they deserve all others.

The problem is that his faith in worthlessness is enough to stop him. Your lack of self-esteem has a direct impact on the likelihood of success simply because self-esteem determines whether you try first. If you do not look dignified, you will not worry because there is no reason to risk everything when you are sure that you will fail.

That is why correcting low self-esteem is so important. Instead of giving your best, you waste everything. It doesn't improve because you don't see the value of doing it, and it's not right for you or you. If you want to get out of this problem once and for all, you must take risks. Self-esteem is one of the primary human motivations, and people should be able to earn the right amount if they dare to expect them to be the person they would like to be. If you want to be successful, happy, or generally reap the benefits, you should be able to say that you respect yourself enough to give yourself the chance to succeed you want.

For example, suppose you want a new job. You found the perfect one: has hours and needed payments. It has benefits that will significantly help your family. It is the passion you are passionate about. You are qualified for work. It's a unicorn job that's perfect for you, and you're sure you'll love it if you get hired.

However, instead of being excited to find this job, that would be all he wanted, and he is petrified. Look at the list of tasks and feel that it would be impossible to get it. You know you want to work, but you don't think work loves you.

Your doubts are activated. A voice deep in your mind begins to whisper all kinds of lies to scare you away from being used. Instead of being sure that you can get a job, you begin to convince himself of all the reasons why you should not worry. You tell yourself you're too stupid. You tell yourself you're not friendly enough. You say yourself that you are too young or too old, or that you do not have the right attitude. Instead of gathering the question, resuming, and preparing for the conversation, you turn to doubts and self-pity, and this leads you to difficulties in arranging the problem. An hour before closing the job application, you must hurry to send the request and send something that was randomly run at the last minute. Of course, she doesn't get a job because she didn't have time to check the details, and her application was full of all kinds of typos, errors, and, in general, rush. So you remember why you didn't waste time earlier this week when you would have the time you needed; you didn't see any points because you didn't get the job anyway. This kind of logic is terrible; over time, however, he could make sure that he was free of errors. You could have done several editing series to make sure that you wrote correctly. You could prepare everything, conduct an investigation, and make sure you know exactly what you are talking about instead of wasting time. Instead of cooking, he spent time wondering why he would not qualify for work. The time spent telling yourself that you don't deserve it could have been enough to make sure you at least received the interview, but now you'll never know.

Determine healthy self-esteem

When your self-esteem is healthy, it usually has some characteristic features that are difficult to fake. You will feel much more comfortable about who you are as a person, and because your self-esteem will have a direct impact on the way you should treat yourself or yourself, it can become quite obvious when you have such a person. Let's take a moment to review some of the characteristic signs of a healthy level of self-esteem.

You have confidence: because your spirit is directly related to how you perceive yourself when you have healthy self-esteem, you'll find that your mind also increases. You can say what you like and don't like it. You can say what you want to say. You will not be afraid to risk and risk, even if there is a possibility of failure. Your self-assessment will prepare you, and you can trust yourself and your skills.

You can say no: when you don't trust yourself or when your trust is low, you usually try to prove yourself. But when you strengthen your self-esteem, you have the strength to tell people " no," if necessary. Don't be afraid of the consequences of telling people that you can't do something or that something will not work. Don't worry about disappointing others because you think you are doing the right thing.

You are positive: when you have more confidence in yourself, you are much more likely to remain positive. Instead of hearing that the world ends when something goes wrong, you can remember that you can try again in the future. You can keep exercising and do better in the future. You can ask other people when you are more prepared. You can learn from your mistakes.

You are immune: with healthy self-esteem, don't worry if you fail. You may be disappointed, but it is not enough for you to feel that you should avoid trying in the future. It doesn't have to be perfect: you know that it sometimes fails, and you accept it. You recover when you fail and become stronger. Don't let anything stop you.

You can express what you need: sometimes, especially if you don't trust it, it can be challenging to show what you need. However, with high self-esteem, you are not ashamed of your needs or feel that, for some reason, you should suppress them. You can accept that you must act according to your needs to make sure that you meet them and you are sure to do so.

## Benefits of healthy self-esteem

Remember that self-esteem has some freedom, but most of the time, it remains within the scope dictated by current self-esteem. This range is too low, healthy, or too high. When your self-esteem is healthy, you gain all sorts of privileges and benefits.

## You have healthier relationships

Thanks to your healthy self-esteem, you'll find that your links are becoming more robust. You will not feel the need to impress others or to change yourself, which means that it can be desired of who you are with. The higher are your chances of finding someone who is compatible. AR yellow part of this may be desired can so want an express what you need. This will prevent the build-up, let ę you and contempt, which could face problematic relationships with other people. You also recognize that you are worthy of basic human decency, which means that it will not tolerate other people, but smokers behave to you as Obey has elapsed.

Your expectations are realistic.

When your self-esteem is healthy, you can recognize that nobody is perfect. You can keep realistic expectations because you know you don't have to be accurate, and you know that others will not be perfect either. It means that you can start to adapt your expectations to others and yourself. It will not require more than common sense.

You feel good with yourself

When you have self-esteem, you are not afraid to be yourself. You are not scared that people will evaluate your choices or preferences or that you are not worthy, which is why you feel that you can express yourself. You show the world who you are, and you don't care if the world dislikes it. The only person you have to love is yourself, and you agree with it.

You can deal with misunderstandings

With healthy self- respect, you can recognize the difference between someone you disagree with and don't like him. You know that people may not accept what you are doing without actively hating yourself.

Uncertainty doesn't stop you

Doubt is no longer terrifying when you have good self-esteem. You know that you can handle almost any situation and trust yourself. You know that you can overcome adversity, and this gives you confidence.

You do not feel that you need approval

When you have such high self-esteem, you don't think that you need the support of the people around you. Instead of applying for this consent, you can verify yourself and your self-esteem. You know that you are good enough for yourself and do not be discouraged. You know that your value is not committed to what others think about you so that you can live properly.

# Chapter 3: Factors that influence self-confidence and self-esteem

## Factors affecting self-confidence

Confidence increases over time. When you learn new skills, you have more confidence in them. Although skills increase your confidence, these are not the only factors at stake. Here are some other things that affect trust:

• Having a positive self-image

• Your world perspective

• Ability to deal with errors and criticism.

• How people around you see you

Although self-esteem and confidence are two unique features, some strategies can be used to boost growth in both areas. However, some other techniques may be more effective in growing one or the other. We strongly recommend that you read all the chapters because each of them helps to create a fundamental element of personal development. It will help you increase your confidence, take advantage of new opportunities, try new things, and gain self-esteem in building positive relationships and making smart lifestyle decisions.

Factors affecting self-esteem

Self-esteem is something that develops over time. When you are young, self-confidence is something externally satisfied. People like school friends, siblings, parents, and other relatives with whom you are close play an essential role in how you feel about yourself. When they give positive feedback, it helps develop self-esteem. Similarly, the way they treat you affects how you think about your impact on the world.

One of the reasons that some people are struggling with self-esteem is that they have not received the positive support and support they needed to know their value in the world. Children with low self-esteem still fight only as teenagers. Even if they get the approval of their peers, they can again fight their parents' judgment or criticism. Many factors affect self-esteem when you are an adult. This includes:

• Your perception of others.

• How others see you

• Way of thinking about others

• Professional or school experience.

• The presence of a disability or illness.

• Religious or cultural traditions.

Within these various factors, their thoughts and position are most controlled. You will notice that many of the strategies given to increase self-esteem focus on changing your thoughts and perception of the world around you. This allows you to switch from within.

Chapter 4: Self-Confidence vs. Self-Esteem

Although the terms are used interchangeably, when we talk about how you feel about yourself, there is a difference between self-confidence and self-esteem. They are similar enough, but the concepts are different enough to justify the presence of different sentences, and you must understand precisely what is going on when everyone is talking. This chapter will focus entirely on discussing what self-esteem and self-confidence are before comparing and contrasting them. When you recognize the main differences between them, you can start using the right terms when you talk about your sense of your own identity, which allows you to be more specific.

## Self-Confidence

Confidence, as already mentioned, is your ability to trust yourself and your skills, as well as to love who you are. You can imagine yourself under certain circumstances and make sure you always make the right decision in your situation. He is convinced that he will make excellent or valuable decisions, and this is enough to keep active in his interest without being overwhelmed by doubts. When you are confident, you can accurately recognize your skills by judging what you can and cannot do based on these judgments. This means that you can evaluate what you can do before doing something and use this assessment to determine if you should do something. Confidence may vary depending on the aspect or situation. It can also change dramatically in a relatively short time. For example, you can feel confident in your math skills, which has always been a good idea. However, you can also feel very suspicious when it comes to being able to write a good book or exercise. It's okay: lets you assess your skills and assign the probability of their effectiveness.

Naturally, you feel safer in some environments than in others.

Self-Esteem

Self-esteem is your feelings for yourself. When you are highly valued, stay in a positive light. You look like someone you like. This refers to how much you want yourself. In particular, you look at yourself as an individual and do not trust who you are. Self-esteem is a kind of precursor of self-confidence while being directly influenced by self-confidence. You can't start trusting yourself without self-esteem. Both are connected in a sophisticated way and interact with each other. Your self-esteem will develop thanks to the experiences you have in everyday life. Her past is based on how she now sees her reading this book. Sometimes it changes, but most of the time, people's self-esteem is relatively stable and is the goal by which the individual sees himself. When you have high self-esteem, you are happy with who you are as a person. You don't judge your skills when you assess yourself; you only like who you are. Have fun, and this is enough to start developing self-esteem later. That's why self-esteem is really what you see when you look in the mirror. If you look and smile or are happy, you can like who you are, and that's healthy. You must enjoy who you are to change your mental health. However, if you don't like it, you may have low self-esteem. Low self-esteem is defined as a lack of self-like. You feel bad, and when you look in the mirror, you may feel disappointed or disgusted. You feel unworthy and incompetent, and you are not the right person. Remember this definition for now: comparison and contrast will be useful.

## Similarities

Thanks to these two previous definitions, you can see how similar they are. Both suggest how you perceive yourself. Both suggest that you look at yourself in your figurative mirror and decide what you think about yourself. This is, therefore, of fundamental importance because both self-confidence and self-esteem are involved in creating your value and how you should assess who you are. When you have confidence in yourself, you trust your ability to make decisions, and when you have high self-esteem, you can trust who you are as an individual: you recognize that you are a valuable person. Both relate to this kind of judgment about you. These similarities mean that both are related to each other. Self-esteem depends on self-esteem, and self-esteem also depends on self-esteem. Like two signs of the same coin, both are fundamental aspects of self-reflection ability, and you can't decide precisely if one is more valuable than the other. However, you can be sure that you can trust yourself and develop both self-esteem and confidence. As you can see, your self-esteem is starting to increase, and you should see that your self-esteem is also growing. This means that you can work on both at the same time, even if one of them improves significantly.

Differences

Despite the similarities, there are some rather significant differences between them. Perhaps the most noteworthy is the fact that everyone focuses on a different aspect of who you are and how you see yourself. While self-esteem is about how you perceive yourself as a person and depends on predetermined self-confidence, it's still a bit different than confidence. Taking care of who you are is a noticeable difference. Think for a moment that when you look at yourself in the mirror, she says, "You know, I wish I could do it better. I feel that I don't try, and I am disappointed that it never seems to take some time or effort to do something with me ... the same. It's incredibly frustrating to me. " Would you describe it like low self-esteem or lack of self-confidence? It can be said that he could consider both of them: he expresses that he is not satisfied with himself at the individual level, which automatically implies predetermined self-esteem due to his focus on the person. However, you also mention skills: you are disappointed that you can't do anything, and you feel freezing in delaying and avoiding doing what you had to do first. This means that it defaults by default. Failure to do the right thing can, first and foremost, make you feel that you can't do anything and start seeing yourself in a negative light. This means that your lack of confidence directly affects your self-esteem.

Although both are undeniably similar, the differences are everything. When you say you have low self-esteem, you say you feel bad. You don't value yourself as you should. You may think that you have no value or that you are not the right person for one reason or another. On the other hand, when he lacks self-confidence, he says he doesn't trust himself with specific activities. Lack of confidence is generally associated with your ability to do something, not how you define yourself at all. You must remember this difference to know precisely when to use each sentence.

You may have little confidence when it comes to being assertive towards other people, but you feel that you are generally the right person. You may think that you are a terrible person, but you know that you are an incredibly competent engineer. You can be entirely sure who you are and feel that you are the right person. You can be awful at sports or even feel bad. There are many ways to combine self-esteem and confidence to determine who you are. In the end, however, you must be ready to think about and discover how you feel.

## Building confidence compared to building self-esteem

In general, it is easier to develop self-confidence than self-esteem. Trust can be built simply by practicing or being good at something. As people progress, people achieve results, and their skills and results lists are continually growing. Although these results generate self-confidence, they do little to improve self-esteem. A person's self-esteem cannot be achieved by building a skill repertoire if these skills do not increase their value.

## Chapter 5: Self-confidence and self-esteem assessment

## Self-confidence assessment

Welcome to the confidence assessment. When preparing for this, make sure you have about 10-15 minutes for uninterrupted operation. Pick up a piece of paper and a pencil or other way to write down your answers to qualify.

You must enter numbers from 1 to 25 on the side of the sheet, and write the appropriate letter after each name.

Note the order of answers instead of just accelerating. Sometimes the order of consent does not change, and you should remember this to get maximum accuracy. As you read each question, choose the answer that best describes you. If you can't decide, watch the visceral reaction and write it down. Often, the visceral response is the most accurate. Try not to overthink things and be as honest as possible. The scoring guide and key to reading the results will be included after this assessment.

1. Expressing my feelings is easy for me

☐ I disagree

☐ I do not agree with a bit

☐    Neither disagree nor disagree / neutral

☐    fine

☐    I agree

2. I think I'm very dear

☐    I disagree

☐    I do not agree on a bit

☐    I neither agree nor disagree

☐    fine

☐    I agree

3. I feel the need to meet the expectations of others.

☐    I disagree

☐    I do not agree with a bit

☐    Neither disagree nor disagree / neutral

☐    Fine

☐ I agree

4. I think people always have hidden reasons whether they want to admit it or not.

☐ I disagree

☐ I do not agree with a bit

☐ Neither disagree nor disagree / neutral

☐ Fine

☐ I agree

5. Communication with others is easy for me

☐ I disagree

☐ I do not agree on a bit

☐ I neither agree nor disagree

☐ fine

☐ I agree

6. I think that I am one of the worst artists of all around

☐   I agree

☐   Fine

☐   I neither agree nor disagree

☐   I do not agree on a bit

☐   I disagree

7. I always know correctly what to do in a conflict.

☐   I disagree

☐   I do not agree with a bit

☐   Neither disagree nor disagree / neutral

☐   Fine

☐   I agree

8. And how a person I am today.

☐ I disagree

☐ I do not agree with a bit

☐ Neither disagree nor disagree / neutral

☐ Fine

☐ I agree

9. I'm afraid to look silly on others

☐ I disagree

☐ I do not agree with a bit

☐ Neither disagree nor disagree / neutral

☐ Fine

10. The worst-case scenario in a social environment is that everyone can see that I am making a mistake

☐ I disagree

☐ I do not agree with a bit

☐ Neither disagree nor disagree / neutral

☐ Fine

☐ I agree

11. When I meet other people, I'm not afraid to be myself, no matter how strange it may be

☐ I disagree

☐ I do not agree with a bit

☐ Neither disagree nor disagree / neutral

☐ Fine

☐ I agree

12. I like to make sure everyone is happy, even if it comes at the cost of who I am or what I want. I am ready to make this sacrifice.

☐ I agree

☐ fine

☐ I neither agree nor disagree

☐ I do not agree on a bit

☐ I disagree

13. If someone is to be unhappy, so should I

☐ I agree

☐ fine

☐ I neither agree nor disagree

☐ I do not agree with a bit

☐ I disagree

14. I consider myself rather shy and afraid to interact with other people.

☐ I agree

☐ fine

☐ I neither agree nor disagree

☐    I do not agree on a bit

☐    I disagree

15. I feel that everyone around me is setting impossible standards that I will never be able to meet

☐    I agree

☐    fine

☐    I neither agree nor disagree

☐    I do not agree on a bit

☐    I disagree

16. It doesn't matter if I do something right, because something will always be wrong.

☐    I agree

☐    fine

☐    I neither agree nor disagree

☐    I do not agree on a bit

☐    I disagree

17. People would hate me if they knew who I am

☐    I agree

☐    fine

☐    I neither agree nor disagree

☐    I do not agree on a bit

☐    I disagree

18. I prefer to defend my beliefs than avoiding conflict. I have no problem protecting my expectations and preserving them.

☐    I disagree

☐    I do not agree on a bit

☐    I neither agree nor disagree

☐ fine

☐ I agree

19. Especially when I do something that affects other people, I make mistakes on the side of indecision

☐ I agree

☐ fine

☐ I neither agree nor disagree

☐ I do not agree on a bit

☐ I disagree

20. Strange that something embarrasses me. I could have fallen, and I still didn't care.

☐ I disagree

☐ I do not agree on a bit

☐ I neither agree nor disagree

☐ fine

☐ I agree

21. Me for myself. They want to use me, and I don't blame them. I wouldn't mind either.

☐ I agree

☐ fine

☐ I neither agree nor disagree

☐ I do not agree on a bit

☐ I disagree

22. I make a significant contribution to my family

☐ I disagree

☐ I do not agree with a bit

☐ I neither agree nor disagree

☐ fine

☐　I agree

23. I am a friend who everyone goes to for help.

☐　I disagree

☐　I do not agree on a bit

☐　I neither agree nor disagree

☐　fine

☐　I agree

24. I get nervous when I am looking for someone else, and I never receive messages from them.

☐　I agree

☐　fine

☐　I neither agree nor disagree

☐　I do not agree on a bit

☐ I disagree

25. I stay late at night thinking about what I did wrong that day and how stupid I saw myself.

☐ I agree

☐ fine

☐ I neither agree nor disagree

☐ I do not agree on a bit

☐ I disagree

The result of the confidence assessment

Congratulations! You completed the self-assessment. Qualifying for this test couldn't be easier: assign a numerical score to each answer, which will be added soon.

Letters must be marked as follows:

☐ 0 points

☐ 1 point

☐ 2 points

☐ 3 points

☐ 4 points

Add the sum of each answer, and you should get a number between 0 and 100. This will help you determine how confident you are as a person. After all, the higher the score, the safer it will be. The vast majority of people will generally score a point in the middle, and those who have less confidence will get lower marks, and those who have a lot of faith will get higher marks. Remember that this is not a diagnostic tool, and you should start by thinking about the result. When your score is ready, go to the next page for information on how you did it and what your score means.

Reading results

0-40 points: low confidence

If you've earned spots in this area, you probably don't have faith. You do not consider yourself valuable, trustworthy, or respectable or accurate trust. You feel that people do not recognize you as a noteworthy person, and you think that it is not worth much to the people around you. You may think that your friends and family do not care about you, and if so, only because of pity and not because you deserve love. He feels that they see him as an act of charity, and that makes him feel worse than ever. You will likely be extremely shy and afraid of something remotely similar to criticism. Try to avoid any confrontation you see and are ready to do everything possible to stop or prevent it. You'll even go as far as giving up your beliefs or options to avoid fighting someone. Compliance is more comfortable than appreciating or commenting on what is happening around you.

## 41-80 points: average self-esteem

This range is for people with average confidence. Of course, this is a relatively wide range of results, which means there are different types of people here. In general, however, you have enough confidence to defend yourself when it comes to pushing. He will be willing to express his opinion and say that he wants things to go in a specific direction. It will come back, however, if you think it is more comfortable, and sometimes they need for adaptation may be more reliable than the desire to protect.

You know your strengths and weaknesses, and you can be kind enough to tell if you are good or bad at something, and that's fantastic! However, he is still overestimated or underestimated often enough not to be sure where he is in the spectrum, despite the general concept. When you are in this area, you can do well with social interaction as long as you interact with people you think are equal and not better. Even if you often don't feel worse, it happens sometimes and can make it difficult to establish meaningful relationships with people around you that seem better.

## 81-100 points: high confidence

This range is limited for one reason: few people have high confidence that is justified and justified. This category is reserved for those few charismatic people who seem to be able to enter and leave social circles quickly. No matter where they go, they trust themselves to be themselves without having to hide anything from them. They have very few or no secrets and have no problem being honest about their true beliefs and desires. A person with high confidence has no problem interacting with people, regardless of their social position, and spends the same time talking to someone much higher in the hierarchy of the workplace, for example, with a partner. They can flow between groups and make it natural. This person will probably defend all beliefs, no matter what. Even a threat is not enough to convince this person to revoke his ideas: he has sufficient certainty about who he is and what he thinks, and no one can take him.

## Self-esteem assessment

Welcome to the self-assessment. When preparing for this, make sure you have about 10-15 minutes for uninterrupted operation. Pick up a piece of paper and a pencil or other way to write down your answers to qualify. You must enter numbers from 1 to 25 on the side of the sheet, and write the appropriate letter after each name.

Note the order of answers instead of just accelerating. Sometimes the order of acceptance or disagreement will change and should be considered for accuracy.

As you read each question, choose the answer that best describes you. If you can't decide, watch the visceral reaction and write it down. Often, the emotional response is the most accurate. Try not to overthink things and be as honest as possible. The scoring guide and key to reading the results will be included after this assessment.

1. I want to bring a lot of value to my relationship

•I disagree

•I do not agree on a bit

•I neither agree nor disagree

•fine

•I agree

2. I think that the people around me love and respect me

•I disagree

•I do not agree on a bit

•I neither agree nor disagree

•fine

•I agree


3. I feel that I should end my desires when I do something socially

•I disagree

•I do not agree on a bit

•I neither agree nor disagree

•fine

•I agree

4. I am still worried about the embarrassment of my loved ones.

•I disagree

•I do not agree on a bit

•I neither agree nor disagree

•fine

•I agree


5. I like meeting new people and meeting them.

•I disagree

•I do not agree on a bit

•I neither agree nor disagree

•fine

- I agree


6. I'm sure I'm doing the worst of all my friends

- I disagree

- I do not agree on a bit

- I neither agree nor disagree

- fine

- I agree


7. I never compare myself to those around me to see how they are doing

- I disagree

- I do not agree on a bit

- I neither agree nor disagree

- fine

- I agree


8. I usually like my company

- I disagree

- I do not agree on a bit

- I neither agree nor disagree

- fine

- I agree


9. I am sure that when I try to interact with other people, I do it shamefully or that it will be discussed later.

- I disagree

- I do not agree on a bit

- I neither agree nor disagree

- fine

- I agree


10. If I had to make a mistake in public, I feel that everyone will remember and judge him.

- I disagree

- I do not agree on a bit

- I neither agree nor disagree

- fine

- I agree


11. I am unafraid of showing people around me who I truly am

- I disagree

- I do not agree on a bit

- I neither agree nor disagree

- fine

- I agree


12. My sole purpose in life is to make sure that my loved ones are taken care of and happy, no matter what the cost for me. •I disagree

- I do not agree on a bit

- I neither agree nor disagree

- fine

- I agree


13. I would much rather be the one suffering than anyone else

- I disagree

- I do not agree on a bit

- I neither agree nor disagree

- fine

- I agree


14. I prefer to spend time by myself, away from sight, because I feel like people are judging my every move

- I disagree

- I do not agree on a bit

- I neither agree nor disagree

- fine

- I agree

15. I feel like I will never be good enough for myself

•I disagree

•I do not agree on a bit

•I neither agree nor disagree

•fine

•I agree


16. I will never be able to make those in my life thrilled

•I disagree

•I do not agree on a bit

•I neither agree nor disagree

•fine

•I agree

17. I am a drain to my friends and family, though they may say otherwise. They are only trying to be polite when they spend time with me

- I disagree

- I do not agree on a bit

- I neither agree nor disagree

- fine

- I agree


18.  I have no problems telling my friends that I do not want or like something

- I disagree

- I do not agree on a bit

- I neither agree nor disagree

•fine

•I agree

19. I would much rather someone else decide what we are going to do so I don't accidentally choose something that those around me hate

•I disagree

•I do not agree with a bit

•I neither agree nor disagree

•fine

•I agree

20. I would much rather someone else decide what we are going to do so I don't accidentally choose something that those around me hate

•I disagree

- I do not agree with a bit

- I neither agree nor disagree

- fine

- I agree

## Self-assessment

Congratulations! You completed the self-assessment. Qualifying for this test couldn't be easier: assign a numerical score to each answer, which will be added soon. Letters must be marked as follows:

a)    0 points

b)    1 point

c)    2 points

d)    3 points

e)    4 points

Add the sum of each answer, and you should get a number from 0 to 100. This will help you determine how healthy your self-esteem is. After all, the higher the score, the healthier your self-esteem will be. The vast majority of people will usually get a middle point, and people with low self-esteem will get lower results, and people with healthy self-esteem will get higher results. Remember that this is not a diagnostic tool, and you should start by thinking about the outcome. When your score is ready, go to the next page for information on how you did it and what your score means.

Read your self-esteem

Self-assessment results in 0-30 points

Very low self-esteem When self-esteem is very low, you probably can't mix with the people around you. You may think that life does not make sense or does not contribute to the people around you. You feel that you are more exhausting to the people around you and that it would be better if your friends and family were without you. The lack of self-esteem is so profound that he thinks that disappearance can be a great benefit to those around him because he can't do anything. You can endure extreme physical, psychological, and even sexual abuse because you don't feel interested anyway. This self-esteem is dangerously low. When your self-esteem is so small, you have a higher risk of harmful or dangerous behavior.

You can seriously use the interaction with the therapist to find a source of low self-esteem. You don't have to live like that.

31-60 points: low self-esteem

In this window, your self-esteem is still quite small, but it has limitations. You will not always tolerate extreme bullying, although you may not notice a problem with some behaviors, such as insults or other emotional abuse tactics. His low self-esteem prevents him from defending most of the time and prefers to remain calm before revealing his needs. When you are at this level of self-esteem, it turns out that you are angry or angry with yourself most of the time. You don't feel it's worth it, and you are not kind to yourself when you make mistakes. It's easier to point your finger and blame yourself for your failures than to make sure you're working on yourself.

## 60-85 points: average self-esteem

In this regard, your self-esteem is quite good, although sometimes you can fight it. You realize that you have sufficient self-esteem not to resist abuse and abuse, but sometimes you do what someone else wants to avoid clashing or discussing entirely. You probably won't argue if you can avoid it, but if you don't like something, you will express your opinion. He may still get into the dangerous habit of looking at other people and confronting each other, but in general, he is much more capable of defense and does not tolerate abuse.

## 86-100 points: healthy self-esteem

When you get a result in this regard, your self-esteem is sturdy enough. You can forgive yourself when you make mistakes, and you genuinely believe that your life adds value to the people around you. You know that you are worthy of love and respect and follow them. He is not afraid to take risks, even if he knows that he may fail. In this range, you can still fight for your life, but that's ok. Nobody is perfect, and you have the self-esteem necessary to face this realization and expectations. You can spend your life more or less unscathed when something goes wrong because you expect mistakes to be made, and sometimes problems arise, and you are hard enough to go on.

## Chapter 6: How to Build Self-Confidence in Yourself?

Now that you have accepted the fact that you can develop confidence let's look at the practical ways you can take on the business of building trust. I will give you a step-by-step approach that will provide you with the results you want if you follow it. Are you ready?

## Step 1. Determining

How many times have you decided to do something to get back to your words and your old habits after a few tries? It is the same with confidence. Everyone can choose to do something, but only a specific person can keep his word. It is usually because, as the saying goes, nothing good is easy. Whatever you do in life will cost you. Achieving confidence will require you some time, effort, strength, and courage, and if you are not very determined, you will return to your previous forms even before starting. It is a determination that will deliberately blind you to all the reasons why you should give up your confidence journey.

## Step 2: Learn from safe people

There is almost nothing you would like to do in your life that someone has not done yet, but maybe different. Even when it comes to learning how to develop confidence, you should also look at people. However, this is not very difficult, and I will show you how to do it. I think you have patterns and people you admire and want to be. Good. Now you can start observing your lifestyle at a closer distance. Study your biography, read their stories, follow them on social networks, listen to them. Their lifestyle will gradually infect you, in the sense that you will begin to learn to face life with the same level of confidence they exude. It does not mean that you should copy other people's lifestyles. A confident person does not imitate other people. The difference is that you are trying to get started and need some direction. When you look at the lifestyle of people you admire and get used to their trust, your subconscious mind will

105

receive a message and will also show confidence. So don't imitate; watch Learn and develop your style.

## Step 3. Attack your fears

Those who don't have confidence lose a lot of life opportunities because they don't believe they have what it takes to go out and do different things. The only way to deal with your fears is to face them ahead, and until you meet them, you'll stay at the same level you've always been. To grow, you must act, and you must act now. What things make your heartbeat every time you remember it? What should you do, but you didn't because you think you're not good enough? You must now get up and start doing them. You may have heard that courage is not about lack of fear, but about the ability to do what you should do with fear. You don't have to wait until you stop being afraid, because this moment will never come. No one has any concerns at any time in his life. Their behavioral patterns and great speakers also have their fears, but today they hear their names because they do not let their concerns determine their actions. To become confident, you must stand up and follow your fears. However, they will always be there, so don't let them stop you.

## Step 4. Permanent practice

Anything you repeat several times becomes a habit over time, and you can start doing it without thinking. The same applies to develop confidence. When you act according to your fears, you should repeat your actions over and over again until they become a habit. In general, if you repeat the same thing for at least 21 days, it will become a habit. Make a list of the main areas of your life where you are late due to a lack of confidence. Choose items from the list and practice them for at least 21 days. You'll be surprised by the result you get. Repetition emphasizes, and when you highlight your skills on your fears, you reduce them, and you will be responsible for your life. Overcoming some fear once is not enough. You have to beat him repeatedly and repeatedly until you undoubtedly believe you are able. For example, if you're afraid of public speaking, you can do something to get out of this fear and build the trust you need to make everything work for you. You can start by standing in front of the mirror in your room and talking alone. If you know that no one else is looking and you are not afraid of being judged, you can try freely. When you speak, turn on the voice recorder on your phone, and record your voice so that when you hear the sound of your voice, the fact that you can speak effectively will be an impulse to continue. After improving speaking in the mirror, you can use the video recorder to record your performance, which you can then publish on social channels. You must feel free and remember that you are not taking part in competitions or anything else; Everything is for fun. When you receive comments from friends online, you will learn their strengths and weaknesses and improve yourself accordingly. If you keep doing this, you won't find that public speaking is as scary as it used to be. After the first real commitment to speaking without fear of the audience, don't relax and think that you've won the battle. You should look for other speeches to have more opportunities to keep the fire going.

Step 5. Durability

Although I show you what you can do to increase your self-esteem, they may seem very interesting to you, and you may want to jump in and start trying them out. Okay, but there is something else you should know it. It is never easy to change from one lifestyle to another. After deciding to be a safe person, learn from other safe people, attack their fears and repeat the process through continuous practice, you need to be persistent in all this and know that even if you want to throw a towel and give up, you can continue your training. It's not easy, and there are times when you will feel depressed. But it must be persistent enough to keep and make it work. Every known person who succeeded had to go through a period of perseverance in small actions, which led to the great success you see now.

Step 6. Positive affirmations

In order not to give up half your confidence, you must have constant reminders in the form of positive affirmations. Keep telling yourself that you can do it. The words we speak are powerful and, over time, are written in our subconscious. Write down a few things you want to see in your life and talk to yourself each day by doing the necessary items to do them. You can write these positive words and place them in strategic points in your room or office, where you will see them every day to remember what your goal is.

## Safe statement

I believe in myself and in my ability to do what I propose. I will keep working on myself until I'm scared. I am the owner of my own life. I believe in myself.

## Chapter 7: How to build self-esteem

Has your self-assessment fallen below expectations? Was there something in the test that surprised you? Even if your self-esteem is low today, you don't have to take it as a permanent expression: it can make your self-esteem stronger and healthier. Thanks to this more energetic and healthier self-esteem, you will feel much better with who you are as a person. You will feel more deserved and stop treating yourself as a second-class citizen who does not deserve attention or care. Developing self-esteem doesn't have to be complicated. In fact, after a few simple lifestyle changes, you'll notice that your self-esteem can and will improve significantly. You will find that trusting yourself in dealing with other people is exponentially easier. When you can successfully treat people, you'll find that you'll be much more likely to tolerate nonsense. You will know when to draw a line and defend yourself.

In particular, there are five simple changes you can make in your lifestyle and thinking that will help you drastically develop the self-esteem you deserve. You must learn to believe in yourself. Confidence in who you are can significantly improve your ability to treat yourself with the respect you deserve. You must convince yourself that you feel comfortable with your skin. You must learn to put negative thoughts aside. They will only serve to support you in life. You must learn to ignore the opinions of others, remembering that other people cannot determine who you are or what you are doing. Finally, you should make sure you choose a positive mindset to eliminate any doubt.

By following these steps, you will find that you are happier in life. You will be able to do much more if you trust yourself. In this chapter, we'll discuss the importance of each of these elements to develop self-esteem is something you can believe genuinely. The other episodes will lead you to this. You will learn to put an end to your self-destructive thoughts, allowing you to convince yourself of self-confidence. You will learn to recognize your value by letting you start ignoring the opinions of others. He will learn to love himself, allowing him to live a life of positivity. You will learn to feel compassion for yourself, helping you stay positive. Finally, you'll get a handful of exercises that will allow you to deal with social anxiety once and for all.

Believe in yourself

When you believe in yourself, you trust. He knows what he wants or needs to do and is sure he will. When you have that unwavering confidence, you can be more productive overall. Thanks to this confidence, you know that you can do what you have to do, and thanks to that faith, you want to take this opportunity. You know that there are no guarantees in life and that you cannot assume that you will always be successful, but trust your skills and judgment, so go as expected. You will not be overwhelmed by doubts and wondering if you can make something work or whether you should try first. When you can confidently and confidently say that you believe in yourself, you say that you believe in who you are. He feels at ease and knows his current skills, and thanks to this knowledge, he knows that he gets along well. The risk doesn't seem so scary.

When you believe in yourself, you see another essential advantage.

Love who you are

Don't be ashamed of who you are as a person, and expressing your tastes and desires is something you do willingly. You know who you are ok with. Your comfort in the skin becomes one of the greatest strengths that you can use to be faithful to yourself regularly.

Self-confidence lets you trust yourself. Because self-esteem and confidence are strictly related, but different, you should make sure you build your self-esteem if you want to have decent self-esteem. This is due to self-confidence. Having this trust is essential.

Of course, confidence is something that can be extremely difficult if you are not ready for it. Sometimes you should make sure you can see that it's worth believing in. If you start to feel uncomfortable, it will be difficult for you to think about yourself. It is only for this reason that you should learn to convince yourself. For most of his life, it is said that it must be realistic. Maybe you've dreamed of being an artist, musician, or even a writer, and everyone around you has always told you that you'll never be able to earn real money by doing all this. They told you stories of a hungry artist, a person who is not able to pay for what he needs. Perhaps you were told that your dreams were too frivolous, and over time you let this voice replace yours. You lost faith in who you were as an individual and lost confidence in yourself. However, this trust can be returned. You can believe in yourself again. You can remember that he can do what he hopes. You can make sure you can take that risk. All you have to do is try.

When you need to convince yourself to believe again, you should learn to recognize these doubts in your mind. Find out what doubts speak to you and learn to fight them. Make them easy. If you feel you can't do anything, remember you are trying. Show how you work to be better and live the best. When you start to alleviate these doubts, you'll find that you have a better chance of listening to yourself. Much of the fact that you can believe in yourself and be able to convince yourself to do something implies the remaining steps in this book. You should be able to reject the opinions of people who are depressing you because they are not doing anything positive for you anyway. You must learn to focus on positive successes and cases where you have been successful. You must be able to trust and love yourself again. You should be able to try, even if you have to try. When you use it all together, it turns out that you can start believing in yourself again. Gradually, the doubt that has darkened your mind will disappear, and you will find that success is much more likely. You will be happier than ever. You will trust yourself more than before. And most importantly, your confidence and self-esteem will increase.

## Give up negative thinking

Negative thinking can be paralyzing. When you think negatively, you may find it almost impossible to overcome these negative thoughts. They manifest themselves insidiously, keeping you depressed. You will feel that you cannot actively do any things you want to do because your negative thoughts will keep you depressed. Whenever you try to do something you want or need to do, these negative thoughts can frighten you and attack your mind, stopping you. When you feel you can't get what you want, you probably won't try.

Because these negative thoughts can make you refuse to try in the future, in the face of the choice between trial and inaction, they can completely paralyze you. When you can't decide to act, you never risk growing up as a person. It leads to failure, and this failure leads to the belief that you can never do what you need. There are many different ways to put negative thoughts aside. You can learn how to counteract them. You can improve them with the help of restructuring and cognitive therapy. You can actively cancel them, rationalizing and weighing the pros and cons. Ultimately, the way to overcome negative thoughts is to find the one that suits you best. You want to be able to work with methods that will be useful to you, and if you do this, you will find that you are incredibly capable. After lifting the veil of negativity, you will be more willing to take risks that will help you grow as a person. After all, the only way to grow is to take risks.

Ignore the opinions of others

When you need to develop self-esteem, the only person you should worry about is yourself. It's easy to feel that you need to confirm who you are and what you can do with yourself, and if you do it regularly, you'll find that it's never good enough. Someone will always think that what you are doing is wrong, ineffective, useless, or simply unable to succeed. There will always be someone who wants to cut you off as a person. If you were listening to this person, where would you end up? The answer is that you'll always doubt yourself because someone still doubts. Even celebrities have people who hate them: no one in the world likes them widely, also if people who don't want them don't like them because of their popularity or something else. This means that the opinions of others always lead to low self-esteem.

For this reason, it's time to put aside what you feel about yourself concerning how others see you. Remember that we are talking about self-esteem, not general popularity. You must be happy with yourself. People who want to do the only discouragement should not hear; Everything you listen to will lower you even more, and this is not conducive to developing the self-esteem you need. If you remember that someone will always have something negative to say about everything in the world and that nothing in this world is universally loved, then you can remember that ignoring the opinions of others is excellent. You can reject what other people think when their ideas are negative and listen to those who mention you. However, you should never determine your value in the way that others see or treat you. It does it sorely: it will depend on other people confirming the sense of security or peace, and this is not healthy.

Of course, ignoring the opinions of others can be difficult. It is hard to ignore the criticism that was thrown in the face, even if they were invalid or invalid in the first place, but learning it is essential. If you can ignore them, you can be sure that you will succeed. You can make sure that the only opinion that matters about you is yours, and with that in mind, you can be sure you trust your judgment. When someone has something negative to say, remember that negativity is not productive. It doesn't help you stay rooted in this negativity, and you can overcome it with the right effort. You can do it All you have to do is focus on the positive aspects that lead us to the last step.

Focus on positivity

When you can focus on positivity, you can always find something useful in everything that happens around you. Has your car broken? You lost a car accident you got stuck in for hours. Have you lost your job Well, there is a better opportunity for you. Have you broken up with your long term partner? Well, now you can find the right person for you.

Instead of thinking about evil, learning to focus on positivity lets you find something that reminds you that everything is all right. You can tell yourself that sometimes you don't mind defeat because failure has a positive effect. When you feel unwell, you remember past successes or cases where you can directly contrast what you think. For example, if you find that you feel entirely incapable at the moment because you have not passed the test, remember that you have already passed the previous test and that if you are studying, you can also pass it.

Diverting attention from negative to positive reminds us that ultimately one negative occurrence does not define it. Avoid being paralyzed by doubt. Keeps these negative automatic thoughts at a distance, rendering them irrelevant or illogical. If you can point out positive cases that directly contradict this negativity, you can help fight these negative thoughts before they can paralyze you. If you can actively fight these negative thoughts, you have the chance for the best self-esteem you are fighting for.

## Chapter 8: Rely on self-esteem to increase self-Confidence

Fortunately, there is a better alternative. The alternative is to work on self-esteem. In other words, you need to work on transforming self-esteem. By building a solid foundation of self-confidence and self-esteem internally, this is projected outwardly onto a growing level of confidence. Will it happen overnight? No. It is that comfortable Well, for some people it is more convenient than for others, but it still requires effort. However, this requires some consistency and constant struggle.

## How it's working

People with low self-confidence have negative opinions about these things. They think their position is basically. They believe they are not worth much. They think that whatever they feel will be mediocre. The bottom line is that they don't believe they are special.

You need to work on your perception. You need to change your understanding of yourself. You must move from seeing yourself as an eternal victim of a situation and circumstances beyond your control to someone who will cause something to happen. It is a huge step forward in self-perception. You pass by someone who sits only passively and watches his life unfold in front of someone who imagines himself as a person who plays a direct role in what is happening. Again, go to the person who comes back and looks frustrated with what happened in your life, and is always wondering what happened to the person who makes something happen.

All this returns to self-perception. How do you imagine? How do you see What is your image of yourself? This perception is crucial for self-determination. By defining yourself, you set your limits. Determine what you are capable of. You represent what holds you back, or that pushes you forward. The best thing about all of this is that you always have control because you decide, not the other person.

Change your narrative

Another critical aspect of working on self-esteem to increase self-esteem is that at some point, you should change the narrative. As mentioned earlier in this book, your description is a continuous story that flows through your mind. It is the organization policy or the history of the organization you are registering with. All their experiences, all interactions with the outside world, and their people are filtered through this narrative. For example, you have the description that you are an unwanted person when you walk in the door, and people look at you with a unique expression on your face; you likely interpret this as a cynical look. I would understand how they see it as merely saying that it should stay away. They don't want you here. Go away If your narrative says that you are a valuable person and that people would be happy if you were close because you have something positive to bring, you will probably interpret the same aspect of the invitation to introduce yourself. Maybe you can treat it as a challenge to create a pleasant print. Anyway; You will find yourself in a completely different place. Instead of feeling small, unwanted, excluded, rejected, and frustrated, you can see it as a neutral contact invitation. I could even consider it a favorable opportunity. Do you see how vital your narrative is? His description is crucial to the way he interprets his reality, believe it or not, all the things we treat as objective truth are judgments. That's all I am. Two people can look at the same set of facts and go away with two completely different interpretations. His narratives determine the difference in these interpretations. When you work on developing self-esteem through self-esteem, you must necessarily change the story. Specific changes must occur in this process for this process to succeed.

Change your thought patterns

An interesting thing about people's perception of reality is that in many cases, their understanding of reality is merely a product of their mental habits. If you usually interpret things in the worst way, it's easy to conclude that this is the only way people can explain these signs. It is the single justice they can have. After all, because it automatically assumes that you receive positive comments or stimuli in a certain way, it must be the reality. Well, you may think that because you have a mental habit. Your mental patterns are set so that you always end up with a specific conclusion. What would happen if you changed your mental habits? What would happen if you changed your thought patterns? Does this necessarily mean that you would end up with the same judgments? There is a good chance that after changing your mental habits, you will have a different perspective on self-esteem and personal value. The most crucial fact to eliminate here is the choice of mental habits. I know that sounds crazy because you might think: Well, I was just born that way. Here's how I feel. You may wonder again why the way you interpret your reality must have come from somewhere. This is something you have learned or learned along the way. Many of us learn about our mental habits from our parents. We also learn this from the people we continuously meet. There is a group thought. If you change a group of friends, you'll be surprised how your mental habits and attitude change. Either way, you must question your spiritual practices. It is something you choose.

It is not something you were born with. This is not imposed on you, and you have no other choice. You always have the power to choose. You can still be aware of and fight your mental habits.

\

# Chapter 9: Development of self-awareness

If you read this book, you probably realize that your life does not go where you want. You may want more, but you are afraid to take steps to get there. You can also ask yourself what your purpose or what is the meaning of life is. In this chapter, we will discuss self-awareness and its relationship with self-confidence and self-esteem. Self-awareness means adapting to emotions, thoughts, and needs. It also means being aware of your motivations and decision models that play an essential role in your actions and how you interact with the world around you. Self-awareness describes a higher level of understanding that helps you be closer together on a deeper level. You start to see obstacles that get in your way, as well as what you can do to overcome them. Living a life of progress and development, you can feel proud and confident in your journey. And, by deciding which parts of your personality you want to shine, you can create the life you want to live.

Signs of low self-esteem

People who live with low self-esteem usually develop it for many years before realizing what is happening. Some may still struggle with the problems they experienced as teenagers. Other people may start struggling with self-esteem in adulthood, trying to build a life that they can appreciate. Regardless of when feelings of low self-esteem start, the first step is to say that you are fighting. Here are some of the most common signs of low self-esteem:

• Continually thinking about negative thoughts about you

• Focusing mainly on its flaws and weaknesses, without intending to inspire change or solve the problem

• Difficulties in dealing with stressful situations

• Fear of failure

• Difficulties in accepting compliments or positive comments

• You need the approval or peace of others.

• You need to establish social status or show good habits to make them look more attractive.

- Difficulty trying new things.

- Behaviors such as promiscuity, drinking, drug use, and impulsive actions

If you have recognized at least 3 of the above practices, you may have difficulty self-esteem. You can also consider your overall feelings about yourself. If you feel confident and have a goal, you probably have good self-esteem. However, if you are unsure of your life goal, you may have difficulty self-esteem.

Signs of low confidence

Lack of trust can drastically affect your life. It affects the people you feel comfortable with and the situations you find yourself. There are many signs of low confidence that include:

☐ You can't leave the house without attaching hair, makeup or preparation

☐ Clear the misunderstandings to avoid conflicts

☐ You often use the phone in social situations

☐ You are hesitant to even when making simple decisions, such as where to eat

☐ You have difficulty sharing your opinion with others.

☐ Has difficulty accepting constructive criticism.

☐ You have a bad attitude

☐ You compare yourself with others

☐ Has a problem accepting compliments.

☐    Easily give in to the goals, and you can't try new things

If you have 4-5 of these qualities, you may have difficulty with confidence. Remember that trust can be situational. For example, you can feel safe at work, but you have problems in social situations.

Be self-aware

Self-awareness happens on levels. Studies show that a person usually realizes how different he is from the people around him after 18 months. Children aged 4 or 5 develop a higher level of self-awareness. At the moment, they understand that their movements in the mirror are their own and can identify in photos and videos. There is also an understanding that they even exist from the perspective of others. This self-awareness lasts a lifetime, but the way it used affects the role of self-awareness in our lives.

## Audience vs. Personal self-awareness

People eventually develop two types of self-awareness. The first type is public self-awareness, i.e., greater awareness of how other people perceive you. Human self-awareness is the reason why people make specific federal decisions to comply with social norms. It is more common when people are in the spotlight, such as when telling stories to friends or presenting at work. When people focus too much on compliance with social norms, it can cause anxiety or anxiety. They may be too worried about how people will react to them, so they remain in social situations and avoid trying new things because they are afraid of people's reactions. If you have too much public awareness, it can undermine your decisions and actions. It hesitantly reduces confidence if alone and self-esteem. Private self-awareness describes how you are aware of yourself. It usually does not apply to physical aspects because it describes internal and personal awareness. These can be physical symptoms such as butterflies in your stomach when you see someone attracting you or panic that occurs when you realize that you have not studied for the exam. Although no one around you can say that your hands are sweating (unless they shake hands physically), you are aware of your nervousness.

## How to use personal and public awareness

The goal of self-awareness is not to become self-aware. You should not put yourself in a situation where you are incredibly anxious, or you question your decisions. Be aware of everything. Consider your strengths and weaknesses. Consider the moments in which you managed to deal with difficult situations and the mistakes that lessons taught you. When considering public awareness, think about how people's perceptions of you affect your relationship and the opportunities offered.

The correct way to use your self-awareness is to use it in a way that improves you. Someone who does not share their ideas in the office because they are afraid of the judgment of others will lose opportunities such as running a project or employing a loud client.

Their boss sees them as someone who does not have innovative ideas or someone who does not have self-confidence and therefore assigns the most essential roles in the organization to a person who believes that he can manage the situation better.

When you become aware of your strengths and weaknesses, you can learn to use these strengths to develop useful skills. Also, find out in which areas you can improve. Better quality relationships are another advantage. When you realize your relationships and what the other person is thinking about you, you have an idea on how to improve your relationship. For example, someone may realize that a mother is sad at the end of her visits.

This perception can make you wonder what's wrong with you: you can be sad because you don't often visit and know that you won't see them for a while.

Finally, self-awareness helps you learn to take care of yourself. Your goals become more apparent when you realize the things that make you happy and complete your goal. The benefits of some relationships in your life will also become more apparent. You will learn which contacts to devote your energy and attention to, and which links distract you from your life or harm your life. You'll have a better idea of what you need to do to reach your goals.

## Greater self-awareness through meditation

Meditation often grouped into spiritual habits or religion. However, regular meditation should not be about religion. It's about discipline. Meditation is a form of mental training that calms down crazy speech that many people think. Think about your last meal or shower. Do you spend business lunch enjoying your meal and taking the break you need to refresh your mind? Or maybe you are thinking about things you want to finish at home before the evening? Are you stressed when you take a shower? Or perhaps you spend time enjoying the warmth of water after a busy day and a pleasant feeling of cleanliness? The average person leads an extraordinary life. It generally believed that if you want to succeed, you must remain involved. There is always something to do, and you often spend time relaxing and worrying about these unfinished things. It is the reality of many people's lives, but it creates an unhappy experience. When you don't give yourself time to slow down and reflect on your life, you don't give yourself time to prepare for self-improvement. So without a specific goal, you may be trapped in the same formula for life.

Benefits of meditating on self-awareness

• Meditation is often called the "path of enlightenment." Self-aware people know each other at a deeper level, which allows them to shape their lives. Meditation based on many principles, especially those used in Buddhism, Taoism, and other religions. The purpose of this meditation, however, does not have to be religious. When you meditate on self-reflection, you look inside to understand yourself because you are the creator of your life. You are the only one who can decide if you are still working without a way out or whether you will take steps to make your dreams come true. You are the only person who can decide if you want to spend the rest of your life with the person you are dating or if you are moving away from the path of life. Here's a look at how self-reflective meditation can change your life.

• Building the foundation of truth: people don't always know who they are at the center of their existence. At other times, they might have departed from their beliefs so much that they lost the sense of what they were. Reflection on meditation helps you see those areas where you have deviated from the value system. It also helps to understand the areas where the course took place. It gives you an idea of some of its strengths.

• Better use of talent. Sometimes, we eventually push the path of life without thinking about what we're good at. Think about someone who has a diploma in art but who works in a factory because it was the first open position they found after graduation. Although they have talent as artists, they are always tired of work and do not work to promote this talent. They'll get stuck in this job, even if they despise it and eventually become loyal to the company. However, they are dissatisfied with their lives, and their passions will be lost. When you think about things that make you happy, it allows you to see hidden talents. By reflecting on these strengths, you can find inspiration for their development and use them in a way that will benefit your life.

• A better way of thinking about goals: when you don't set goals, you move in life without a purpose and direction. There is no pressure to do anything, so it's easy to say it will start "tomorrow" or "next month." However, if you don't stick to it, you'll never see results. Reflection gives you time to think about your goals and the path to achieving them. It also allows you to spend time thinking about the responsibility for achieving the goals and if you are actively trying to make them.

• More exceptional ability to exert a positive influence: only a few negative interactions are needed to achieve a negative reputation. Nobody wants to be marked as "quiet," "strange," or "bad." Unfortunately, people do not always clearly read the characters we are trying to send. Even when you try to be positive, you can see areas of life. When you slow down and wonder, it allows you to make sure that your actions reflect who you want to be seen. It will enable him to exert a positive influence on the lives of people around him.

• A better understanding of the subconscious: the subconscious is responsible for remembering all our memories, thoughts, and reactions to various stimuli. This is why someone who has been abused shudders when his partner moves too quickly during a quarrel, even if that person has never hurt him. That's why someone checks the locks every night after the theft. When you meditate, you have a vision of the subconscious, as well as underlying memories, emotions, and thoughts that can cause unwanted reactions to various stimuli.

• Greater opportunity to prevent self-tampering. Sometimes people sabotage because they don't believe they are worthy of anything. In other cases, they can sabotage because they don't trust their results. For example, a college student may wake up late in the medium term, if he is afraid of failure anyway because he prefers to feel entirely omitted than to admit that he must study more material.

How to meditate for self-reflection

A greater sense of initiation: meditation, if appropriately used, can be extremely inspirational. It allows you to understand the things that held you back and explains your path to your goals. In this way, you become the owner of your destiny and the creator of the life you desire.

During meditation, you must be open to transformation and the thought that you will reveal the truth about yourself. Remember that calming your mind is difficult. This is especially true for people who lead a hectic lifestyle, as well as those who always think. The discipline of the brain is a challenge, and learning it takes time. You may also not be able to keep your mind empty for more than ten seconds on the first attempt of meditation, but this is normal. By continuing training, you'll notice that you can clear your mind for a long time.

One of the best things about meditation is that you can do it anywhere. However, for starters, it is better to meditate in a way that is not distracting. While the teacher can meditate anywhere, achieving this level of mental discipline requires a lot of practice. You should not think of distraction as mere noise or involvement of other people. Disturbance can also be caused by too tight or itchy clothes, or by turning off the phone when trying to clear the mind. Use something comfortable, make sure the room temperature is right and turn off the bell. You should also consider meditation time: meditation just before or after a meal can distract you because you are hungry or swollen.

After establishing the environment, sit in a comfortable position. Traditionally, you sit on the floor, on a mat or cushion, with crossed legs and feet on your thighs. However, this episode can be painful for someone who hasn't done it. It is also allowed to sit on a chair with feet touching the floor or on the floor with crossed legs (but without feet on the thighs). After a comfortable seat, stretch your spine. You shouldn't stretch so that you feel uncomfortable, but you should not lean. The shoulders should be placed directly on the hip bones, and the spine should not be bent.

Now close your eyes and start focusing on your breaths. Count to five, breathing deeply, filling your belly. Then slowly release this breath during the count. Inhale at five. Exhale at five. Now, as you exhale, imagine blowing your thoughts into balloons or clouds. Put all the things that worry or stress you on these balloons and let them float. They may come back to you later, but at the moment, attention clears your mind of all tenacious words that bring worry and stress. Keep breathing while doing this. After all, breathing will become more natural, and you won't have to count. You can still think "inside," "outside," if you want to help free your mind.

When you reach an active state, try to maintain it. Remember that your goal is to stop your mind from being "noisy." You shouldn't worry about your next presentation or what you will eat for dinner. You should expect some of these thoughts to be interrupted. When you think of fear, let your ideas flow. Do not judge this thought or criticize yourself for rethinking it. Learn to free yourself from thoughts that cause anxiety or stress.

Remember that many people struggle with meditation, especially during the first few sessions. It is a good idea to start with five minutes and gradually add when you manage to calm your mind during this time. People who struggle with meditation can improve their results by imagining something in their minds, such as traffic lights or a tree. When the breaths become natural, imagine the object in your account. You have to choose a daily item that you usually don't think about a second. Close your eyes and see the article. Don't think about it or what it is, look at it in your mind. Try to keep your thoughts clear when you exercise them. When you feel at ease, let this object go further into your account. In the end, it should disappear completely. Another option is to observe the flame of a flickering candle or observe the smoke of incense burning during meditation.

# Chapter 10: Is low self-esteem a mental health problem?

Low self-esteem is certainly not a problem in itself, but they are closely related. If many things affect your self-esteem for a while, it can cause problems with emotional well-being, such as sadness or nervousness. Self-confidence, in the broadest sense, is what an individual is worth to himself. Self-esteem identified with the individual's ability to maintain a proper mentality about oneself and to support such positive beliefs in the tested circumstances, especially in situations that require assessment by others. For example, adults with high global self-esteem are expected to have greater prosperity, better social relationships, and greater job satisfaction than their partners. Low self-esteem is identified, for example, with enthusiastic problems, substance abuse, and dietary problems. Although self-esteem is seen as a relatively stable figure, it also varies depending on late setbacks or results, and there are lower levels of self-esteem for specific areas of life, such as sports and extraordinary exercises. Perhaps because of its unusual nature, the idea of self-evaluation was widely discussed in psychological writing. In any case, despite the changed definition, the concept of self-assessment has been extensively studied, in particular in social tests. It has been carefully examined concerning emotional well-being and quality of life and areas such as schools, work, and exercises.

Self-confidence and self-esteem

Beliefs and assessments that individuals have about themselves determine their identity, what they can do, and what they can become. These fantastic internal influences provide an internal control system that guides and supports people throughout their lives and monitors their behavior. Human ideas and emotions about them are commonly referred to as self-esteem and self-esteem. These, along with their ability to cope with the hardships of life and control what happens to them. The concept of self-esteem is characterized as a whole of beliefs and information about his colleagues and personality traits. It is classified as a subjective concept that organizes theoretical and substantive perspectives on itself and controls the preparation of relevant data for itself. Various ideas, such as self-image and self-observation, are the equivalent of one's concept. Self-assessment is simply an evaluative and useful measure of self-assessment and is considered equal to self-assessment, self-assessment, and self-assessment. This refers to an in-depth study of its positive or negative value, referring to the results that a person assesses in various aspects and areas of life.

## Self-esteem as a protective factor

Self-esteem is not only perceived as a basic element of mental well-being but is also a protective factor that contributes to the improvement of well-being and positive social behavior by acting as a buffer against influences, negative. It was noticed that it successfully progresses in stable work, which is reflected in life perspectives such as results, results, results, and the ability to adapt to diseases such as cancer and coronary heart disease. On the other hand, unstable self-esteem and low self-esteem can be crucial in improving various mental and social problems, such as misery, anorexia, bulimia, nervousness, brutality, drug abuse, and high risk. These conditions not only cause high levels of personal torment but also exert a great impact on society. As will be shown, subsequent tests showed low self-esteem as a risk factor and positive self-esteem as a protection factor.

In summary, self-esteem is considered convincing for both physical and emotional well-being; therefore, it should be an essential goal for improving well-being, in particular psychological well-being. Wellness promotion refers to a method enabling people to build authority and improve their well-being. Emotional control, like general well-being, is considered to be critical elements of the concept of well-being. Self-awareness and self-esteem are the two main elements of emotional well-being, and therefore an essential focal point of early psychological well-being. It has been noted that self-confidence is the most common and unbelievable indicator of joy (Furnham and Cheng, 2000). Although low self-esteem causes personality disorders, positive self-esteem, basic principles, and goals seem to contribute to "well-being effectively,"; Self-esteem, personality, and trust are some of the basic elements of emotional well-being. The resistant element of self-esteem is most evident in studies that check for stress and physical illness, in which self-esteem manifests as protecting a person from fear and vulnerability. It is reflected in the perception of constantly sick people. It was found that a strong sense of authority, vitality, and high self-esteem, in addition to having a partner and many close relationships, has a direct defensive effect on improving depressive symptoms in still sick people. Self-esteem has also been shown to improve a person's ability to adapt to illness and postoperative survival.

Negative self-esteem

Low self-esteem can lead to a decrease in gratitude, generation of self-destructive mentality, mental impotence, social problems, or dangerous practices. It is an important perception because there is a motivation to accept that self-esteem should be analyzed not only as a cause but as a result of problematic behavior. For example, from children, they may have a negative look at themselves, which can cause sad emotions. On the other hand, discouragement or lack of competent work can cause a terrible feeling that can reduce self-esteem.

Negative self-esteem is also seen as a critical factor that causes madness and even moderation. Without confidence, people become unable to deal with everyday problems, which limits their ability to achieve the most extreme potential. This can lead to a weakening of physical and mental well-being. A decrease in emotional well-being can lead to problematic disguise behaviors such as pain, anxiety, and dietary problems. People with high self-esteem have made internal attitudes more solid and global for constructive occasions than for adverse circumstances, which has strengthened their constructive mental self-configuration. People with low self-esteem were subject to adverse events related to permanent and global internal attributes and positive opportunities for external variables and happiness. In longitudinal tests, low self-esteem in childhood, adulthood, and early adulthood were considered an important indicator of misery in later life. When cumulative stress, social support, and self-esteem were adequately presented in the recurrent study of the last two, only self-esteem was a critical depression.

The primary role of self-evaluation in school years is explicitly included in the study of dietary problems. At this stage in life, weight, body shape, and calorie counting behavior are related to personality. Analysts have revealed that low self-esteem is a risk factor for developing eating problems in young students and adolescents.

Also, low self-esteem appears to be cautious due to the unfortunate outcome of treating such a problem. The critical impact of self-esteem on self-perception has led to the development of programs in which the development of self-esteem is used as an essential tool to prevent eating problems. In summary, there is a standardized relationship between self-esteem and the inclusion of problematic behavior. Besides, there is sufficient evidence for the future to recommend that low self-esteem may increase the integration of problem behaviors, and improved self-esteem could prevent such disintegration.

Although the reasons for these practices are diverse and unpredictable, many scientists have identified self-esteem as an essential factor in the fight against misconduct, health, and social change. Interestingly, low self-esteem, as well as high and swollen self-esteem, is associated with the improvement of disturbing symptoms. Low self-esteem and negativity can hinder the acceptance of duty and useful criticism, which can block him from the circumstances and even prevent him from facing new challenges; therefore, avoid satisfying meetings for a lifetime. It can also destroy significant connections. Low self-esteem, which affects our feelings, thoughts, and behaviors, and also shows how we perceive ourselves and interact with other people and us, can happen for some reason. The reason is the denial of the people you defend, keeping your precious slave in circumstances that are not under your control, and if they don't go when needed, you will feel like a failure and some mental problems, such as personality disorders and killing. Seven tips that you can use to start gaining self-esteem and be the person you pretend to be.

Chapter 11: Basics of low confidence

Can you tell the difference between high and low morale? Well, it's pretty easy. People who describe themselves, their results, relationships, and all other associations in a negative way may have little faith. Yes, we all do it at some point in our lives, but only people with low self-confidence think about it regularly. With low self-esteem, we want to say that these people generally have a negative view of their skills, assess and negatively evaluate their results, and criticize themselves. They have a negative and rigid belief about others and themselves. These opinions are sometimes treated as facts or truths about them that ultimately hurt their personality and life.

## Causes of low self-esteem

Although your opinions about yourself may seem like objective statements, they are just opinions. The truth is that the experiences you have had in your life shape your opinions. These experiences allow you to understand your nature and personality better. If you have had negative experiences, your opinions about you also appear to be negative. The most important experiences that shape our opinions about ourselves, usually, but not always, occur at an early stage of life. What you see, hear, and live in your childhood has a significant impact on how you view yourself. Many times negative opinions about you can also be caused by the experiences you have in your next life. For example, bullying or harassment in the workplace, persistent difficulties or stress, traumatic events, or offensive relationships are also a cause of poor self-discipline among people.

refusal

Low confidence can develop when a person feels rejected by family, friends, colleagues, teachers, etc.

Inappropriate treatment

If someone is bullied or ridiculed in childhood, they can develop thoughts such as "I'm stupid," "I'm just not good enough."

It is expected to meet high standards

A person who always tries to meet the standards or expectations of another person is unlikely to show confidence. Constant criticism of parents, colleagues, colleagues, and others can also lead to this negative feeling.

You feel different from many other people

people think that they are not adjusting, especially in childhood and adolescence. It has a severe impact on how they perceive. At the moment, physical appearance is essential for most people. Thoughts like "people don't like me because I don't look good" or "I'm not beautiful enough" can become real opinions that get stiffer over time.

No positive people

Those who grow up in an atmosphere of breathlessness, feeling, warmth or praise, generally have no confidence. For example, if the child's basic needs met, but his parents showed no physical or emotional feelings, the child may become a less secure person.

Disturbing life events

People who experience traumatic or stressful events are angry with others. They can also react negatively. Relationships, pain, or health problems are some of the factors that can harm self-confidence.

Abuse, abandonment or punishment

If a child is neglected, mistreated, or unjustly punished, he may think negatively about himself. The same applies to adults who may have brutal relationships.

Personal effects of low confidence

Low confidence can seriously affect how people perceive themselves, their skills, and their talents. Influences are also on the way they work in everyday life. He adds he discusses some of the possible effects of low self - confidence in a person's personality:

☐	They can say a lot of things about himself disheartened. It is difficult for them to accept compliments.

☐	They feel guilty, restless, frustrated, ashamed, or depressed.

☐	They criticize themselves, their skills, and their actions.

☐	They always think that they will never feel right.

☐	They doubt, blame themselves, and humble themselves.

☐	They focus mainly on the mistakes they have made or the results they could not make.

☐    They are never able to recognize their positive qualities.

## Impact on everyday life

The above-mentioned personal items have a severe impact on everyday life. Read the list below to find out how a person with low self-esteem works in their daily lives:

Their fear of failure allows them to avoid stressful situations. Because they have a negative opinion about their skills, they do not reach their full potential. They believe that their previous successes are the result of luck, not their qualities and abilities. It also affects your relationships with family, friends, or colleagues. For example, they may try to please others, avoid social interactions, become extremely shy or shy, or feel overly anxious or upset about any disapproval or criticism. You can also see a significant change in their appearance. While some people who lack self-confidence do not attach much importance to personal hygiene, others try to hide their perceived weaknesses, paying particular attention to their appearance. They may not even look directly into the eyes of others if they think they do not look perfect. Low self-esteem also has a significant impact on food or alcohol consumption. While some people may follow a strict diet, others may start overeating.

# Chapter 12: To achieve a higher level of confidence

Since you've read everything about how amazing it would be to trust yourself, I'm sure you're wondering: How can I develop a better level? There are many different ways to do this. Women must live peacefully. There is a famous saying: "Life is 10% of what you do and 90% of how you do it." You will probably often come up with all these scenarios and think about how unbelievable the task can be if you are sure. Well, trust is not something that can come overnight. It takes time, but the sooner you start, the more differences in your personality you will notice. It will be like developing a completely new version of yourself! Start implementing the following tips step by step in your everyday life, and you will not be disappointed. Instead, when you leave the other end after completing these tips, you'll be a completely different and confident man!

## Understand your strengths and weaknesses

Of course, you can't be amazing in all your life skills. Maybe as a girl, you feel more comfortable in modeling, but you are not a good athlete. So, according to this advice, you should focus on your secure areas. The more time you invest in your strengths, the better! Don't waste time hitting the bush and try to learn new skills by improving those you already know.

Remember that people don't always trust everyone. Most of the time, they pretend, and you also have to learn that. But don't worry, you'll get the most out of it! Discover your strengths and weaknesses. Take the last from your life and gain confidence in your powers, grinding them as much as possible.

Take responsibility for yourself

This is an essential component of the confidence formula that you can't put aside, no matter what. As a woman, you have to start taking responsibility for yourself. Try to forget about the people around you for a moment. Try to focus on becoming a better version of yourself. Try to perform even the smallest tasks for yourself. If it's a phone call for someone, do it yourself. Work on your communication skills. If you want to buy something online, you prefer to go to the store and meet the sellers.

When you work and find a steep path, take responsibility. Do not give up; Try to find solutions to fix the mistakes made. Similarly, if you have achieved a fantastic result, take responsibility! Tell others in the workplace and be appreciated. He finally feels happy; You deserved it.

Use humor

If you still don't know, find out now. When something confuses you, don't let others know you. Use humor and get out of the situation! Humor is also a symbol of trust. Everyone can be honestly serious, but you need the confidence to take the situation and change it into a light mood through humor. Besides, it's not a joke; People love girls with a good sense of humor.

However, you don't believe it? Researchers at the Harvard Business School have found that people who feel free to tell jokes and have a good sense of humor are much safer than others who prefer to keep fun away from work.

So, girls, it's time to understand the nature of the people around you and encourage them to make funny jokes, because humor is the way to a safer life.


Get ready to do your homework

You need to prepare for the homework. First, start devoting some time and investing your time in things that will help you take confidence to the next level. At the top of the list, you should prioritize your work and complete the tasks assigned to you. This is because the more activities you organize and carry out, the more experience you'll have at work. Experience leads to trust! If so, in the future, there will be more action or similar tasks you can perform with the utmost confidence. So yes! A tip would be to prepare yourself for any task that comes along the way: don't leave work halfway. Manage your time effectively so that you can master the art you practice, and eventually, you will gain more confidence!

Develop an action plan and follow it.

The best way to get things done and stay current is to develop an action plan. It's like a to-do list but will focus more on how you want to do tasks and do things that will increase your safety. Action plans are a great way to stay motivated while traveling! Plan one that applies to your professional or personal life and make sure you do it entirely and do not leave it halfway.

For additional motivation, look back and see how far you have travelled since you started acting as planned. Think about all the positive aspects that will appear when you gain all the trust you need! The trick is that when you implement your action plan, you already gain confidence because you believe in yourself enough to follow the plan you set yourself!

## Stop thinking that your ideas are stupid

How will you know if your ideas are good if you never talk about them? It is time for you to reject this quiet voice in the back of your mind that is still depressing you. Your idea may be the best of all the people who sent it, but if you never talk about it, how do you find out? And don't be shy if your idea is rejected, it gives you more space to think about how to improve. It is a step towards trust! Trust yourself and trust your opinions. Introduce your ideas to others. Tell your thoughts If they appreciate you, that's fantastic! It's a natural way to strengthen trust. And even if you didn't, at least you tried. Next time, you'll say more and come up with much better ideas!

## Recognize your role models

Look around and find women and even men in this case that will inspire you. Think about your behavior, kindness, trust in your tasks, and ask yourself, do you want to be like that? Look for people who are trustworthy, reliable, and have a lot of confidence because they believe in themselves! If you want, you can also identify some of your favorite celebrities. However, finding a model from a loved one can give you a motivating impulse to be like him. You will see them every day, and they will continue to inspire you to do better things.

## Surround yourself with the right people

Low self-esteem usually begins in life because it does not like influential characters. For example, if you are constantly informed that you are not equally or criticized for everything you have done, you can prevent him from becoming a brave adult with a positive mental attitude. To build your boldness, try to surround yourself with constructive and reliable people who recognize and strengthen your positive qualities, such as your commitments, and who strengthens you.

## Get to know yourself, even more, / Become the best friend

Regardless of your differences, you are necessary, and you have the right to love yourself. Therefore, spend time alone and take time to get to know yourself, which will allow you to find out if it is unique, exceptional, and commendable, allowing you to get a higher rating. You can also try to make a list of your achievements and features that will help you remember, and then review it at any time that needs self-esteem and needs to feel better. It is also an amazing time to identify and deal with any negative perspectives that you have towards yourself.

Recognize where you need to change

We all have problems; However, if you do not realize and admit where you need a change, you can take it in terms of low self-esteem, which will worsen when you try to get away from it. Instead, think about and recognize where you need to change and then set the power to improve it. You can also sign up for the help of a good friend or relative. You should also worry if you judge yourself too much and then advise you that these are not realities that will help you keep a strategic distance from negative feelings that can cause negative internal dialogue.

Try not to compare yourself with others:

 psychotherapists warn that these correlations only lead to negative mental vision, which can lead to low self-esteem, stress, and nervousness that can destroy your work, your connections, and your physical and psychological well-being.

Repeat positive affirmations

Similarly, as negative affirmations, as if you were an idiot, you may believe it and not even believe it. Therefore, therapists recommend repeating positive affirmations that you must accept about yourself every day to help you advance smoothly up to the period before low self-esteem. Studies show that positive affirmations can even help reduce the side effects of misfortune and others. Managing easy things like cleaning, combing hair, wearing clean clothes, good nutrition, and exercise often help you feel good. Studies also show that a comfortable, perfect, and attractive living space also helps to improve the layout. They offer donations, volunteering, and help other, less happy people, not only help to eliminate the concentration of their problems, but also make them feel great when they realize that they are helping other people. Research shows that achieving more things in life that you can be happy with increases your self-esteem, which makes you feel better.

Finally, people with positive self-esteem are open to progress and more meaningful experiences, which means they do not depend on external fortifications, such as status or salary, for self-esteem, which allows them to find more satisfaction and enjoy their life experience. Pay attention to the people you allow in your life, as well as the conditions that will enable you to decide about self-esteem. You should also take care of yourself, even exercise, and eat properly to help maintain a stable body and mind.

## Find a mentor

If you know someone confident enough to take risks one after another and want to cross your boundaries and be brave like her, then maybe you should talk to her at some point and tell her about your struggle with confidence. Yes! Ask him to lead you. Ask him to help you overcome these struggles and instill in you the same trust. Finding a mentor can help you; it's like someone is always monitoring you.

## Chapter 13: Great habits to increase self-esteem

"The strongest relationship you'll have will be with you," Steve Marble

What should I do to build self-esteem?

To develop your self-esteem, you must challenge and change your negative beliefs about yourself. This may seem like the most difficult task, but there are many options you can try to help.

## Do something you like

Doing what you want and where you are perfect can help build morale and increase self-esteem. You can achieve this through incentives offered as a reward for work; Provide free services, comments, or hobby classes.

## working

Work can give you a solid personality, relationship, habit, and reward. Few people develop in a difficult situation and appreciate the work of achieving their goals. Other people consider work as an unfavorable task or unpaid voluntary work. Whatever you do, it's important to feel determined and strengthened in your career, and that the harmony between work and family life is right for you.

Hobbies activity

It can be anything from learning a new language to singing and an art course. Think about where you think you have some natural features or things that you have wanted to try for a long time. Try to discover exercises that are not a big challenge for you so that you feel that you have achieved something and had the opportunity to develop your morale. Online schools, libraries, and adult schools should contain the subtleties of the clubs and neighborhood classes you should attend. What makes me feel more positive is doing things. When I see what I have done, and I like it, I think consistently good because I think I discovered something I am good at.

Try to create positive connections.

Try to connect with people who do not scan you and with those who are ready to talk about your emotions. If you invest energy in constructive and stable people, you will have a better vision of the mind, and you will feel more determined. As a result, if you are careful and compatible with other people, you will probably receive a positive response from them. It will allow you to feel good about yourself and the way other people see you. If you have low self-esteem, there may be people near you who stimulate negative beliefs and assumptions. It is necessary to highlight these people and take steps to stop them from doing so, perhaps by greater confidence or time limitation, interacting with them.

Learn how to be assertive

Being assertive means respecting yourself and other people, and talking with respect. This will help you set clear boundaries. The following will allow you to act more decisively:

• Pay attention to non-verbal communication, as well as the words you say: try to be open and confident.

• Try to express your feelings if someone bothers you - wait until you feel calm and explain clearly how you feel.

• Say no to absurd demands.

• Tell people if extra time is needed or help with difficult tasks.

• Try to talk to the first person, if applicable, for example: "When you talk to me like this, I feel ...". It allows you to reveal what you need without looking honest or scared.

Assertiveness can be a difficult feature to learn, and you may need to try it out by talking in front of a mirror or with a partner. Numerous adult education institutions, such as schools and universities, also offer assertiveness lessons. There are also many self-improvement tutorials with practical exercises and available tips for buying or using the Internet.

Take care of your physical well-being

Taking care of your physical well-being can allow you to feel happier and more useful, as

201

well as improve your mental image. Exercise improves health feelings and self-image. Exercise releases endorphins, hormones, to "feel better," which can help improve your mental state, especially if you do it outdoors.

I stay

Lack of rest can cause false emotions to be misrepresented and suggest that you may feel less secure, so making sure you have enough rest is essential.

diet

A balanced diet with standard meals with lots of water and vegetables will help you feel healthier and happier. Stopping or limiting alcohol consumption and staying away from tobacco and recreational medicine can also help improve overall well-being.

take the challenge

If you set goals and work to achieve them, you will feel satisfied and happy when you reach your goal and gradually feel positive with yourself. Make sure that the configured test is realistic and easy to do. It doesn't have to be important, but it must be important to you. For example, you can write a letter to a local newspaper or start regular gym classes.

Learn how to recognize and challenge negative beliefs

If you improve your self-esteem, you can also reveal your negative opinions about yourself and your background. This can be a complicated procedure, so it is essential not to hurry and ask your partner or partner for help. If you feel worried, you can request an expert for help. It can be useful to save notes and questions, for example, they can help organize your thoughts:

• What do you think are your faults or defects?

• What negative things do you think others think about you?

• If you could summarize, what word would you use: "I am ..."?

• When did you start feeling that way?

• Can you indicate a meeting or occasion that might have caused such a propensity?

• Do you think you always have specific negative reflections?

Keeping a journal of ideas or recording it for several weeks can also help. Write down the details of the circumstances, how you felt, and what you thought was a belief.

Focus on positive things. If you have low self-esteem, you may need the practice to get used to thinking more positively about yourself. One way to achieve this is to make a list of things you like about yourself. You can join:

• Things about your character

• Things about how you look

• Things you do

• Skills you have created.

Take your time and look for 50 unique things, regardless of whether it takes a long time. Keep this list and check another piece every day. If you feel depressed or stressed during an upcoming occasion, such as a possible employee meeting, you can use it to remember things that are beneficial to you. If you can't think of a list of valuables, you can ask your partner or partner to start work.

It can also help you see how others may have greater feelings for you. Another method is to register at least three things that went well or achieved that day before rest. Some also find it convenient to store items such as photos or letters they like.

## Try awareness-raising methods

Consciousness is a method of focusing on the present, using systems such as contemplation, breathing, and yoga. It has been shown that it helps people become more aware of their reflections and emotions, making it easier to monitor them than to be dominated by them.

What can you do to love this help?

When you meet people with low self-esteem, you can do what matters most.

Show them that you care, promise that they will defend you, and take care of them. You can show them how nice it is, listen carefully and even spend time with them.

Help them remember positive things: even if they can't transform the antagonistic image of people about themselves, it can help to question it, helping them remember that they are beautiful works, such as beautiful things or positive things they've done.

Stop blaming others: people with low self-esteem are regularly burdened with negative meetings, including problems with mental well-being. Promise them that this is not their mistake and refrain from leading them to "recover."

Try to be persistent: low self-esteem usually develops for several years. Changing someone's assessment can be time-consuming, and you may need constant comfort. Tell them that from time to time, you can feel awful, no one feels happy and always determined, and they mustn't feel compelled to satisfy absurd desires.

Be responsible: if your partner or family member participates in a self-improvement program or sees a consultant, be healthy and positive. You can also offer generous support, such as looking after children so that they can go to meetings.

Help them find the right treatment: If you are worried that low self-esteem causes mental well-being, train your partner or relative to find the proper treatment.

Personal resources to improve

Remember these main tips so that you can build self-esteem.

- Do the exercises you like.

• Be helpful and accommodating to other people.

• Try not to compare yourself with other people.

• Try to train regularly, eat well, and rest well.

• Be firm: don't allow people to treat you without respect.

• Use self-improvement guides and sites to create support similar to assertiveness or awareness.

• Learn to question your negative beliefs.

• Recognize your positive qualities and the things in which you are perfect.

• Get used to remembering and saying positive things about yourself.

Self-esteem is an idea to some extent; It's difficult for someone who doesn't need to recognize what it looks like. One way people with lower self-esteem begin to acknowledge what appears to be higher self-esteem is to think about how they will feel about what they hold in life — for example, many people like cars. Because vehicles are necessary for them, these people consider their cars. They use common sense where to leave the vehicle, how often to repair it, and how to drive. They can connect the vehicle and proudly show it to others. This is self-esteem, except that you love, care for, and enjoy. When children accept, they are meaningful and valuable; They consider themselves. They use good judgment about themselves, which increases their value instead of breaking it.

Increase your confidence with body language

Body language is one of the most important tools for communication. It is estimated that communication is 70% nonverbal or even higher. In other words, what you say with your mouth is much less important than what you say about your body. You can talk, but if you stoop, it will cause anxiety and confidence. The good news is that even if you don't feel safe, practicing a safe body language can increase your self-esteem and make you feel better. Your brain and body language are constantly communicating with each other. And this communication is a two-way street. One at the end of the body language reflects the thoughts and feelings that arise in your mind. But at the same time, your thoughts and feelings are affected by messages that the brain receives from body language. This means that by adopting a positive body language, you can become a more confident man. How do you solve body language? To learn how to use this psychological phenomenon, read the following tips for building trust through body language.

## 1. Smile to be happy

A smile is probably the safest thing you can do. Do you want to see yourself more safely while walking? So smile as you go! Do you want to look more confident when members of the opposite sex stick out in the bar? Smile across the room, and you will not only look friendly but also as if you were happy that you are sensitive, which makes you look relaxed and confident. A smile makes us safer because of the psychological phenomenon is known as "face coupling." This means that we often feel as if we seem. Smile, and you will feel happier. Grimace, and you feel angrier. This special smile releases serotonin, which leads to well-being. Even if the smile is forced, it still works!

## 2. Attitude

Body language communication with the brain is not limited to messages sent from your face. Your brain collects messages from the whole body to determine how you should feel. So, if you want to feel more positive and secure, you should also send confidence messages from the rest of your body. To send these messages, keep your head up, your shoulders tilted forward and backward, and your back straight as if a rope stretched from the base of the spine. At the same time, relax your muscles and concentrate on slow breathing deep into your stomach. Adopting this posture while breathing deeply and relaxing the muscles will send confidence signals to the brain. As a result, you will start to feel more relaxed and confident.

## 3. Walk with confidence

communication with the body language that we discussed in the game is always there, even while walking. Our walk says a lot about us, and if we go fast, with strength and pride, we can give the impression of self-confidence, wonderful and responsible, before we even talk! On the contrary, if we go down, bend, and pull at the legs, we will look shy, closed, and scared. To go higher, the often-described trick is to imagine that a ray of light comes out of your chest. This means you are walking with your chest slightly raised, and it means you should smile and walk quickly. The problem is remembering to do it! Many of us have been walking fairly regularly for ... well, a year! For him so difficult to leave these years of rooted training and start walking in a completely different way. One way to avoid this is to look for triggers that remind you. One of the best is to go through the door. The next time you cross the threshold, use it as a way to remember this trick and start broadcasting again.

## 4. Strength positions

Just as a smile can work backward to change your emotions, body language also affects how you feel. When we trust, we usually take more space. You may not understand that when it takes up more space, it seems more secure. Why? Because it causes the testosterone hormone to increase, testosterone is the primary male hormone, as well as the neurotransmitter that increases aggression and assertiveness. Psychologists managed to find so-called positions of power. These are positions that you can run with your body, thanks to which you will immediately feel safer and on top of the world. The most famous of them is the position of victory. Just keep your hands on your head in an av-way, just like when crossing the winning finish line in a race. It is a universal position, and it is something that people do in all cultures; it is believed that monkeys use this signal to demonstrate victory and success! And apparently, it causes an immediate increase in testosterone levels. So next time you have a conversation or make an appointment, try to go to the bathroom first and train the power!

## 5. Open your body language

Keeping your body language open is another way of transmitting body language to send a message of trust to your brain. Keep your hands with you and do not use them to cover yourself (avoid crossing your arms or drinking a drink on your chest). Crossing your arms is a defensive position and sends signals to your brain that you need to protect yourself. However, keeping your hands to the side tells the brain that you have nothing to fear. In addition to keeping your arms without crossing, do not cross your legs when standing. Instead, stand with your legs apart (hip-width to shoulder) and keep a solid and solid base. Don't be afraid to take up some space and have space around you. Adopting this type of body language transmits a sense of strength and power directly to the brain. Another trick of body language is trying to rely on various things. If it leans against the wall, it means ownership. Similarly, if you touch someone on the shoulder, it conveys a kind of property that is also presented as trust.

## 6. Gesturing

Speaking of the most charismatic people, science also has something to say about it. Studies have shown that people classified as the most charismatic also gesticulate more often. Gesturing means talking with your hands, it means being alive and orientation, gesturing and walking while speaking. The reason for this is trust and charisma because it makes us seem more involved in what we are saying. Now our body language and words are compatible; that's why our passion can be felt in peace. The more you act when you speak, the more passionately and firmly you appear to be what you say. And this is very attractive and impressive: it makes everyone perceive it as more attractive and interesting!

## 7. Avoid negative body language

Your brain not only receives positive body language communication signals. It also comes back from negative aspects. So, if you allow yourself negative body language and uncertain, you communicate to the brain that you should feel bad and insecure. Negative feelings will appear and be strengthened every time you maintain a negative body language. With so much, they not only accept the safe and positive body language above but also avoid the opposite body language. If you frown, lower your arms, drag your feet or become "small," pay attention and immediately apply the opposite behavior. It will help you evoke more positive feelings and gradually get out of this negative mental state.

## 8. Don't worry

Anxiety is a clear sign of nervousness. A man who cannot stand still is a worried, tense, and undoubtedly unreliable person. Your hands can be your worst enemies: fight to make them stable and firm. You can talk with your hands but keep calm and control. Also, while sitting, avoid violent leg vibrations produced by some men (you don't want to look like a dog rubbing your belly). When we are nervous or stressed, we all calm down thanks to some non-verbal and self-destructive Tokyo behavior: we rub our hands, bounce our feet, drumming our fingers on the desk, playing with jewels, turning our hair, we become restless, And when we do one of these things, we immediately steal our credibility claims.

## Chapter 14: How to build physical strength and how it affects their level of trust

Your mind and body are often seen as separate entities, but in reality, they are almost inseparable, and the effects on which one will affect the other. For example, if you are sick and take a fake medicine called a placebo, you can often feel better because you think the medicine will do you good. Similarly, if you are very stressed, your body reacts by increasing your blood pressure. Your body and mind are inseparable, so an increasing number of experts agree that people exercising are less prone to depression and other mental health problems. People who work regularly have more confidence and self-esteem. There are several reasons for this. These reasons include:

1. Increased hormone production to stay healthy

Serotonin and endorphins are formed during exercise and cause relaxation and happiness after training.

2. Increased energy

Although exercise is physically intense, and energy is enhanced by increasing blood flow to the brain and muscles. This can increase mental clarity and creativity, increasing process productivity.

## 3. Look good, feel good

Being unhappy with your appearance will lower your image and confidence. Exercises allow you to sculpt your body and lose fat, so you like what you see when looking in the mirror.

## 4. Sense of success

Even if you want to exercise, there may still be a battle to finish training, and most people are happy when it ends. This commitment rewards him with a great sense of fulfillment that will cover other areas of his life.

## 5. Less stress, stress

can lead to feelings of fear and regret, often demolishing your self-esteem. Exercise is one of the best ways to fight stress. With less stress in life, your self-esteem can develop.

## 6. Exercise is self-sufficient

Most of us spend days doing things to others. We work to pay off mortgages, settle matters for our children, and cook meals for our families. Time spent exercising is self-sufficient because it is only for you, and it gives you a break in doing things for others. This time only you and your training count.

## 7. Exercises increase physical reserves and mental strength

exercise doesn't get easier, as getting in shape can only do more. Your muscles, heart, and lungs become more efficient, and greater physical capacity will facilitate many daily activities. Do you want to take groceries or heavy equipment at home? You don't have to ask for help; Do it yourself with your newly developed muscles! Besides, if you have the mental strength to conduct demanding training, you can apply this hardness to other paths of your life. Do you feel tired because you had to spend all night to meet deadlines? No problem: you were more tired after training. It strengthens and then increases self-confidence. Knowledge of great strength and efficiency is like having a secret weapon or a superpower. Imagine how confident you are if you know the muscles under the suit are tense, the abdominal muscles are strong, and the heart is large and strong.

## 8. Better time management and organization

Adjusting the exercise to an already very intense schedule can be difficult, but with good time management and organization, even a very hectic daily routine can withstand regular workouts. Time management and organization are important skills. If you can make the most of your time, you'll be late or panic less often, which is good for your self-esteem.

## 9. Better posture

Access to the computer keyboard throughout the day can lead to poor posture. People with a bad attitude often seem suspicious. Thanks for strengthening the appropriate muscles, the posture will be upright. It will radiate confidence waves, and if you seem confident, then you will feel it too. You will also have less back pain. How to start a training procedure If you are starting to exercise, it is important to start gradually and correctly. Incorrect behavior can delay for months, causing unnecessary pain or injury, and even putting it off completely. Follow these tips to make sure your first workout is not the last!

## 10. Begin slowly and gradually increase

While it is good to get excited about exercise, exercising too soon can cause severe muscle pain and fatigue. At best, this means you will have to wait a few days for recovery before you can train again. In the worst case, you can completely deactivate the exercise. Gradually relax in the new training regimen. 15-20 minutes of low or moderate-intensity exercise will benefit a lot from the exercise.

When you train and get used to the exercises, you can do more and more exercise.

## 11. Love what you do.

Exercise is not a form of punishment. You should improve not only your physical health but also your mental health. For this reason, it should be excellent. If you don't like your training, it will bother you, and you will even give up altogether. Don't worry too much about choosing the perfect workout. Instead, focus on finding the exercise you like. That way, you will be more with him.

## 12. Learn ropes

No matter what type of exercise you do, you will probably come across new learning skills and techniques. Don't try to run before you can walk; Make sure you study the ropes so you don't make many time-consuming mistakes or even injuries. Buy books, browse the Internet, or rent a bus. Become an expert in this field so that you feel confident and more potent than nervous and confused.

## 13. Mix It

Fitness consists of several physical characteristics that include strength, cardiovascular conditions, endurance, flexibility, and balance. Although specializing in only one or two of these areas is exceptional, you will do more for your health if you combine your workouts to get a full physical state. For example, it's not good to have the strength of an ox if you can't catch your breath while climbing stairs. Similarly, you may be fit enough to run a marathon, but if you are so weak that you can't take your briefcase from the car to the office, your workouts are not very balanced.

## 14. Go ahead!

Being fit and healthy is a continuous process. You are suitable as the last workout. To be in shape, next time you should do a little more exercise. If your workouts stop, your fitness levels also. If you want to change your body, you also need to change your workouts.

15. Train hard, but also train wisely.

Exercises give results only if you do it regularly. Long breaks between workouts will undo many of the hard-earned benefits. However, there are times when losing a workout, or at least taking it easy may be better for you. For example, if you do not feel well, you are injured, you are very stressed, you do not eat or sleep properly, or you feel out of place, a day off from exercise can be better than strictly following a training regimen.

16. Track your progress One of the things that do exercise so enriching is how your body can change. However, these changes are often minimal and easy to miss. After all, you see yourself every day and a kilo less fat here, or

some other muscles can smoothly go unnoticed. Track your progress so that we can celebrate your improvements. Before and after photos, a weight chart, hip, hip and thigh measurements, and fitness and strength tests are an excellent way to track and review your progress.

236

## Chapter 15: Self-Confidence Meditation

Meditation is another fantastic tool to improve safety. Many people are reluctant to allow meditating, thinking that in some mystical way or only associated with the religion and philosophy of the East. This is not meditation at all. Instead, meditation is simply an act of concentration: consciously choose the way you want to direct your attention and decide what to focus on. We have already seen how reflections and worries can cause us to fear and undermine trust. Meditation allows us to determine what we want to think, which may include not thinking about anything. Often meditation is to calm the mind and free it. After healing, you can separate from your thoughts or eliminate them at any time. The next time you panic about public speaking, you can rise higher and put aside incredibly intense anxiety. Meditation also includes breathing exercises, which is one of the most effective ways to overcome stress. This is because our breathing is closely related to our response to stress and our sympathetic and parasympathetic nervous system. When we are stressed, we breathe faster to deliver more blood to our muscles and brain. When we slow down this breath, it has the opposite effect and helps us return to a calmer state called "rest and digest." Over time, research shows that practicing meditation can help us be calmer, happier, and more logical. We can rise above things that don't matter and focus only on things that matter. Not only that, but it increases the dominance of slower and quieter brain waves. And it increases the thickness of the cortex and the number of neuronal connections in the brain. In short, meditation is also perfect for your intellectual abilities and performances. So, contrary to popular belief, the benefits of meditation are immediately apparent in varying amounts. Meditation from time to time is fantastic, and you will see a change with each session you do. However, regular daily meditation practice is the key to experiencing the full strength of benefits that grow exponentially.

How to start with meditation

The following four meditation techniques will help you clear your mind and focus on visualizing trust. They will help you implant new belief systems in the subconscious mind and help you think and act with confidence

1.Conscious Meditation

Mindfulness meditation is the practice of cleansing the mind and focusing on nothing but here and now, without trying to change anything and without judging. Daily participation in this practice allows you to control stress and anxiety. The more you work on it, the stronger your awareness and resistance will be. When starting a conscious meditation routine, it's best to start with shorter periods and slowly increase its duration. You also want to practice meditation at the same time every day. The more you train regularly and continuously, the better your results will be. These are the steps to start practicing daily awareness meditation.

Step 1: Find a comfortable place to sit or lie down. Often sitting is better because you fall asleep less often.

Step 2: set the clock. When you start your practice for the first time, it is best to continue the session for about ten minutes. However, you can extend this time if you feel you can have a more extended course.

Step 3: start taking quiet breaths. Pay attention to how you breathe through your nose, lungs, and nose. Note how the stomach or chest rises and falls with each breath. It is important not to change your breathing or judge. Breathe normally and focus on breathing and body.

Step 4: Then, you want to do a body scan. Start at the top of the head. See how it is. So go to your face. What does the back of the eyelids look like? How do lips, nose, and chin feel? Continue this process by moving your whole body. Pay attention to the feeling and temperature. Look for tensions or tensions in your body, but don't try to change or correct any of your feelings. This process is simply about realizing your feelings and continuing.

Step 5: After completing your body scan, pay attention to the sounds around you. Make a note of your body sounds first. Can you feel the breath? Focus on this sound. Focus on the sounds in the room. What sounds are there in space? Then switch to sounds from the area. What sounds do you hear? Finally, focus on the noise outside the living space. You hear something

Step 6: Finally, pay attention to how you feel now. Let the thoughts floating in your mind float in the air again. Do not judge yourself based on falling from the state of consciousness and do not judge the thoughts that enter your account. Do not attach any emotions to anything. Focus on every feeling.

Step 7: If you find that one of the techniques works best for you, do the rest of the session using this technique, otherwise "be" until the stopwatch sounds.

2.Breathing Meditation,

This technique helps to focus and calm the mind by physically relaxing the body. As with mindfulness meditation, we recommend setting the timer so that you can focus only on your breathing without worrying about the weather. When you feel overwhelmed, this technique can be advantageous. Exercise is easy because you can do it anywhere. To prepare for meditation practice, you can lie down or sit in a chair with your eyes open or closed. For more profound relaxation, it is recommended to sit or lie in a quiet place with your eyes closed. Breathe deeply into your stomach and breathe out completely until all the air in your lungs is empty, ensuring that every breath is rhythmic and constant. During this technique, breathe in deeply until the belly rises and exhales completely as the stomach collapses and pulls. The duration of each breath is not as important as consistency during the session.

3. Visualization

This type of meditation practice will allow you to imagine confidence in all situations. You can use the display before any significant event that causes anxiety or use it every day to help you build trust over time. Follow the steps below to start the visualization exercise.

Step 1: Begin the session with calm and controlled breathing cycles. Focus on breathing until the body and mind relax.

Step 2: Once you relax, say the following mantra: "I have confidence," and I feel that confidence takes over your whole being.

Step 3: Imagine creating a transparent and protective bubble around you. It's a shield that nothing harmful can enter. Imagine you are safe, radiating self-esteem in the bubble.

Step 4: imagine your day ahead of you. Imagine being able to feel confident in any situation protected by this bubble of self-esteem. You walk with your head raised, you communicate with confidence, speak firmly, and never doubt yourself.

Step 5: Imagine every situation by continuing to be self-confident. You see that you always know exactly what to say. Others see you as a confident and successful person. You are full of happiness, positivity, and security.

Step 6: Continue this process until you have passed any upcoming events. End the meditation session with the statement: "I will live this day, radiating self-esteem and maintaining peace in all situations." So the key to proper display is always the visualization of what you want as if I have already achieved. Instead of waiting for success or building trust that will happen one day, live and feel that it is happening today. On one level, you understand that this is simply a psychological trick, but the subconscious mind cannot distinguish between what is real and what is imagined. Your subconscious will work on the images you believe in, regardless of whether they represent your current reality

## 4. Anchoring

is a neurolinguistic programming technique that serves to evoke a mental or emotional picture. It is a condition that arises when a person evokes a feeling and combines it with some gesture or touch. To practice this technique, you must enter into a state of meditation. To begin, use awareness, breath, or any combination. So you want to come up with the emotion you want to condition; it can be success, trust, relaxation, or happiness. Now imagine the moment in your life when you experienced the desired feeling. If you want to feel safe, think about a moment in the past that you trusted. Maybe it was when you got the highest grade in the class or when your high school football team won the state championship. Imagine this moment right now and experience the emotions as if they were taking place today. Feeling your feelings, keep your index finger and thumb together. Relax for a few seconds, then return to imagining a better mood, then fold your thumb and forefinger. Repeat this process three to five times. By repeating this exercise every day, when you put your thumb and finger together, you'll finally experience the same emotions under all circumstances. You can use this technique to renew your thinking. For example, if you anchor a sense of trust, whenever you experience a feeling of overwhelming or doubt, you can use this anchor to stimulate a positive and safe state. Anchoring can also be used with other visualization techniques. For example, after establishing an anchor, you can check your confidence in current or future activities. Engage the anchor by merely placing your index finger and thumb together and experience an emotional confidence response, making the visualization more real

How to meditate for self-reflection

A greater sense of initiation: meditation, if appropriately used, can be incredibly inspirational... It allows you to understand the things that held you back and explains your path to your goals. In this way, you become the owner of your destiny and the creator of the life you desire.

During meditation, you must be open to transformation and the thought that you will reveal the truth about yourself. Remember that calming your mind is difficult. This is especially true for people who lead a hectic lifestyle, as well as those who always think. The discipline of the brain is a challenge, and learning it takes time. You may also not be able to keep your account empty for more than ten seconds on the first attempt of meditation, but this is normal. By continuing training, you'll notice that you can clear your mind for a long time.

One of the best things about meditation is that you can do it anywhere. However, for starters, it is better to meditate in a way that is not distracting. While the teacher can meditate anywhere, achieving this level of mental discipline requires a lot of practice. You should not think of distraction as mere noise or involvement of other people. Disturbance can also be caused by too tight or itchy clothes, or by turning off the phone when trying to clear the mind. Use something comfortable, make sure the room temperature is right, and turn off the bell. You should also consider meditation time: meditation just before or after a meal can distract you because you are hungry or swollen.

After establishing the environment, sit in a comfortable position. Traditionally, you sit on the floor, on a mat or cushion, with crossed legs and feet on your thighs. However, this episode can be painful for someone who hasn't done it. It is also allowed to sit on a chair with feet touching the floor or on the floor with crossed legs (but without feet on the thighs). After a comfortable seat, stretch your spine. You shouldn't reach so that you feel uncomfortable, but you should not lean. The shoulders should be placed directly on the hip bones, and the spine should not be bent.

Now close your eyes and start focusing on your breaths. Count to five, breathing deeply, filling your belly. Then slowly release this breath during the count. Inhale at five. Exhale at five. Now, as you exhale, imagine blowing your thoughts into balloons or clouds. Put all the things that worry or stress you on these balloons and let them float. They may come back to you later, but at the moment, attention clears your mind of all tenacious words that bring worry and stress. Keep breathing while doing this. After all, breathing will become more natural, and you won't have to count. You can still think "inside," "outside," if you want to help free your mind.

When you reach an active state, try to maintain it. Remember that your goal is to stop your mind from being "noisy." You shouldn't worry about your next presentation or what you will eat for dinner. You should expect some of these thoughts to be interrupted. When you think of fear, let your ideas flow. Do not judge this thought or criticize yourself for rethinking it. Learn to free yourself from thoughts that cause anxiety or stress.

Remember that many people struggle with meditation, especially during the first few sessions. It is a good idea to start with five minutes and gradually add when you manage to calm your mind during this time. People who struggle with meditation can improve their results by imagining something in their minds, such as traffic lights or a tree. When the breaths become natural, imagine the object in your mind. You have to choose a daily item that you usually don't think about a second. Close your eyes and see the article. Don't think about it or what it is, look at it in your mind. Try to keep your thoughts clear when you exercise them. When you feel at ease, let this object go further into your mind. In the end, it should disappear completely. Another option is to observe the flame of a flickering candle or observe the smoke of incense burning during meditation.

257

# Chapter 16: Expand your social trust (overcome social anxiety and be bulletproof)

We all want people to love us, but for this to happen, we must improve our social trust. Being able to make new friends and feel safe with strangers is very important for self-esteem and emotional well-being. But many things can stop you. And among the most common problems in this area is social anxiety.

## What is social anxiety?

Social anxiety is the fear of negative judgment and judgment that causes feelings of inadequacy, inferiority, self-awareness, shame, humiliation, and depression. Social anxiety prevents people from expressing their ideas and temperament, and they are generally not understood. People with anxiety disorders experience significant emotional stress in the following situations:

☐ Introducing yourself to other people;

☐ Laugh or criticize;

☐ Being the center of attention;

☐ Observation while doing something;

☐ Meet talented people;

☐ Most socializing, especially with strangers;

☐ Go around the room (or table) over and over, and you have to say something;

☐     Interpersonal relationships, whether they are friends or romantic;

This list is certainly not a complete list of symptoms, and other feelings are also associated with social anxiety.

Where does social anxiety come from?

Today's experts share some ideas from previous decades, believing that most cases of social anxiety disorder are not the result of a lasting event, but that social anxiety is the result of several probable causes. These may be environmental and genetic factors. These are some of the most critical factors that lead to social anxiety disorder.

1. It has been shown that by disrupting social anxiety due to genetic roots, it develops in family lines. Recent studies have shown that this is not only learned behavior, but it is almost certainly also genetic.

Overly developed tonsils

The amygdala is the part of the brain that responds to fear. When it is too developed, it leads to a greater tendency for anxiety disorders.

The level of serotonin unbalanced

Serotonin is a key brain chemical that regulates emotional states. When insane social anxiety can become the result. This may be due to natural causes or may be unbalanced in the past by drug or alcohol abuse.

Family conflict

The history of family conflict, especially at an early age, is one of the most common social factors known to cause anxiety disorder.

Bullying

It is one of the environmental factors that has recently been the focus of attention because it is known to aggravate the social anxiety of young people, which sometimes has very tragic effects.

History of sexual abuse or extreme torture

Sexual abuse and other severe abuse often leads to a more severe end to anxiety disorder. In many cases, this type of experience requires multiple levels of therapy to address not only the most significant social anxiety but also other effects of this trauma. Sometimes its root can be difficult to determine. Fortunately, the methods used to treat it proved useful compared to others.

How to overcome social anxiety through cognitive restructuring

Cognitive restructuring essentially means that you "reprogram" the way you interpret events and the way you think about future events. Cognitive restructuring consists of two main elements. These are "demanding thinking" and "hypothesis testing." Disobedient thinking means that you look at what you visualize and what you say to yourself, and then restructure your mentality by questioning these beliefs, testing them to verify their integrity. For example, you can tell yourself that if you talk in public, people will ignore you, and you will seem stupid.

But now ask yourself:

☐ Aren't these people your friends?

☐ So is it likely to be ignored?

☐ Would it matter?

☐ If they are not your friends, will you see them again?

☐ Isn't it better to at least try?

Currently, the probability of social exclusion and management in nature is improbable. This means that you can talk safely in any environment, no matter who you are! And remember that we tend to increase risk and minimize rewards. Be honest with yourself and rational, and usually, you can reduce fear and anxiety. Meanwhile, the hypothesis test means that you will test the theory and prove that there is nothing to fear. Prove that you don't have to worry about making fun of you. So it could mean that you intentionally said something stupid to see how people react. What if you say something in public and then stutter?

You'll find that most people are patient and forgiving and will respond by merely waiting for it to end. They will also give you great support. In short, testing hypotheses means facing the anxiety with a raised head and saying that they are not so bad. Moreover, they repeatedly face their fears. By repeatedly exposing yourself to scary scenarios, you can become insensitive to fear. If you continue to speak in public, you'll find that you'll normalize it eventually, and it won't be a big problem anymore. You can practice in several ways:

1. If possible, start conversations with strangers.

2. Talk to bidders: be intentionally uncomfortable or weird in places you don't have to go back to!

3. Ask people their number, file complaints, if you are not satisfied with the customer service, participate in lectures, comedy, lectures acting, or singing.

4. Whatever you have to do in front of people.

5.    Do it all, and it will be calmer over time.


You won't react to a fight or flight when you talk or perform in public, and you'll gain more confidence. People assume that it means that you have absolute confidence in what you do or that you are secretly rich or extremely torn. But you learned not to worry about trifles.


## How to make an excellent first impression


This is especially important because these first impressions mean a lot. The way he affects someone when he first meets him has a significant impact on his overall safety, respect, and meaning in his eyes. Practice making an excellent first impression. This means walking the powerful and radiant stairs in the room and means shaking hands firmly and intentionally. If you want to look confident and make a first impression, there are a few things worse than a slow, lazy handshake fish!

1. Eye contact

Another critical element in creating a good experience when meeting someone for the first time and building trust is to maintain proper eye contact. Maintaining eye contact suggests that you feel the same as the person you are talking to and gives you more intensity, makes you look more honest and, in other words, sends all those right social signals we want to send! Therefore, try to maintain good eye contact, but do not disturb.

Hold your eyes for a few seconds, then look away while gesturing, and then keep looking. When you're talking to a larger group, look around and remember to make eye contact with each person for a few seconds.

2. Speak slower One of the things that will help you feel more confident during communication is talking slower. We are naturally inclined to accelerate when we are nervous, which can lead us to stumble over our words and seem less confident and less confident in what we are saying. Of course, this is not a good thing! On the other hand, if you speak more slowly, you will find yourself as someone who knows what he is talking about, who trusts who he is and who thought about what they were talking about. Because

time is given, you'll be less likely to stutter or pause, and you'll have to use um, fill in words.

## 3. Tell stories

Storytelling also conveys trust. And it works together to speak more slowly. One of the reasons we jabber when we speak in public is a faster ending. Let's talk soon why?

a) Of course we don't like public speaking, and we want it to end and

b) We are not sure if what we are saying is convincing or exciting enough, and we are worried that people will stop listening if we do not finish what we are saying quickly.

But if you tell a story, it suggests you are more natural when it comes to maintaining the court and entertaining the crowd. Recommend good fun and trust your ability to entertain. This effect is even stronger if you slow it down. Not only in terms of speaking but also delivery. This means that you are preparing the stage, asking rhetorical questions, using repetitions, and creating tension. This is something that most charismatic people can achieve tremendously and have a significant impact if correctly done. Take your time, enjoy the moment, stay, and trust how interesting you are!

## 4.Nobody is better than you!

And you are no better than others. You're different. You are fantastic, but that doesn't mean you're better than others. This does not mean that others cannot be great in their way. Your size does not take away the size of others. We have been educated with the mentality that others who have a name, a particular social position, or even more effective are better than us, and we must admire them. Today everything goes so fast. Titles and status don't matter so much anymore. For example, there are many people with higher education or even a PhD for the unemployed; On the other hand, some of the best companies in the world were created by people who did not finish school or even high school.

On the one hand, individuals lose their social standing, while others go up. They're different, but that doesn't mean they're better than you. Keep this in mind.

5.Re-connect with friends to build self-esteem

Perhaps you are wondering what friends have in common with confidence? Each of us has moments of doubt and uncertainty. We are very concerned about our appearance. Many times you wonder if you said the right thing or did the right job in a given situation. Sometimes it doesn't matter how to match a dress to the right pair of shoes or a shirt with the right tie. Like any other person, when I am not sure about these things, I ask my friends for a second opinion. You may have noticed that some people play a significant role in building our trust. It is thanks to friends that we can get rid of the skepticism or uncertainty that we have towards each other. It is thanks to them that we can make better decisions in life. Here are some ways in which re-connecting with friends helps build our trust:

## 6. They rejoice for their success

If there is someone you call when you have good news to share, he is your friend. Friends are among the first groups of people to whom we can turn when we have problems, frustrations, or failures. The main reason is that they are proud of what we do. They are people who encourage us and believe in us that we can do it! Knowing that someone is supporting you will help you deal with anything with such confidence.

## 7.Models new ways to be

A proverb says that no man is perfect. However, with friends, they also have strengths and abilities that help them achieve better results in what they do. I have a friend who touches the crowd with his speech. At one point, I was wondering if I could do the same. Thanks to the model you can admire, it's much easier to achieve your goal. By merely modeling his speech, I finally improved. The same applies to you; Having a friend helps us see how we can use his strengths to improve our weaknesses.

## 8. They support our efforts for the benefit of development

Did you know that sometimes the only thing that stands between you and your success is your mentality? Well, the reason he has cold feet in implementing this business idea is that his thoughts tell him he can't do it. However, when you surround yourself with positive friends, they can see strengths in you that you never knew existed. This will give you enough motivation to try, and you'll realize that you only need a small push to fly like an eagle.

## 9. Our tears are dried

There will always be holes in this journey called life along the way. The exam may fail, lose the tournament, be abandoned or worse, lose a loved one. However, when you have friends, you can rely on someone who is depressed. They will be there to provide information from a different perspective. They will bring a lot of sun in the darkest moments.

## 10.They teach us the value of teamwork

Trust is not only working alone. The idea is to know how to go the road alone and when to do it with the team. Sometimes, when you are alone, you may feel shy and uncertain about visiting places, trying new things, or doing different things. However, if you do these things with a friend, then suddenly, a wave of energy appears, and you realize that you can be creative. It allows him to fly higher than he expected. The truth is that the best part about reuniting with friends is that feelings are mutual. They are people who share our dreams, and we can do the same for them. Therefore, surround yourself with real friends and see how it affects your approach and confidence to go beyond borders.

## Chapter 17: How to effectively use affirmations for solid trust

Assertions are statements of internal dialogue and are best presented to the subconscious. These new images are perceived by the subconscious as "credible" and placed in the area of the psyche, which has to do with the power to improve the ability to extract particularly strong memories with less work effort. With these particular images, a person can develop internal tools for the right way of thinking to gain confidence, enabling memories and pictures to be transferred to the here and now, where they are used to improve the way of thinking, which is crucial for a specific trust. Affirmations can help you change negative behaviors or achieve the right mindset, and may also help in the removal of damage caused by the harmful scripts, those things that repeat themselves, which increase the negative perception of themselves and affect our success. Now that you understand the importance of affirmation, let's see how to use it to get the best result with minimal effort.

How to use affirmations

An effective way to use statements for a particular trust is to write them on your card and read them throughout the day. The more often you practice them, the deeper your new beliefs will be. The best times to review complaints are the first thing in the morning, during the day, and at bedtime. But let's see in more detail how to maximize efficiency by following these practical tips: use affirmations during meditation. After relaxing in a deep, calm, and meditative state of mind, imagine that you already have confidence and know-how to cope in any situation. Imagine the environment or physical environment in which you want, in a home that you like and find comfort, attracting many people in your life, and receiving recognition and the appropriate financial reward for your efforts. Add any other details relevant to you, such as the promotion you want, the people you want to meet every month, etc.

Try to feel that this is possible; Experience it as if it was already happening. In short, imagine what it would be like if it were already! Try to stand in front of the mirror and use affirmation when you look into the eyes. If you can, repeat them with passion. It's a powerful way to change your limiting beliefs very quickly. If you find it hard to believe that a statement will occur, add "I choose" to the report. "For example, I want to have more confidence" or "I choose the promotion." Record with voice and play it while you sleep. Some people swear by this technique. Attach positive emotions to your statements. Think about how you will achieve your goal, or think about how nice it is to know that you gain more confidence. Passion is a fuel that strengthens affirmations.

If you don't want people to know about your declarations of trust, place your reminders in strategic places. Remember, however, that it is essential to see them often; otherwise, it will not help you. If you repeat the words of your statements, instead of focusing on their meaning, change them. Of course, you can still say the same goals or features, but reformulating claims can regenerate their effectiveness. Well, now that you know the best ways and times to use affirmations, the next step will be to create your instructions. Here we explain how to do it.

Create your affirmations

Consider your positive attributes. Get to know the list of your best features, skills, or additional features. Are you an expert in meeting new people? Write. Are you a good speaker Give me that. Write each element in a short sentence, starting with 'I' and using the present tense: 'I am an expert in meeting new people,' for example, or 'I am a good speaker.' These statements are statements of who you are. We rarely revolve around things we like about ourselves instead of stopping at things we don't like. The list will help you interrupt this cycle, and using these statements to appreciate who you are will provide you with the security you need to accept complaints. Think about which harmful scripts you want to neutralize or which positive trust goals you want to achieve. Affirmations can be constructive in counteracting the negative perception of your ability to trust in a new company or to succeed. Affirmations can also help you achieve specific goals, such as meeting new people or achieving business success. Make a list of your goals or negative opinions you want to change.

Give priority to the problem list for action. You may find that you have many goals or need many different statements. However, it's best to skip several accounts at once, so choose the most important or urgent ones and work with them first. When you see improvement in these areas or reach these goals, you can make new statements about other points on the list. Use positive affirmations only as a counter-script or add other declarations to model your self-confidence behavior in the future. The instructions you will use to shape future changes should have the same form.

They must start with "me" and be polite, clear, and definite. There are two forms of forward-looking statements that can be used to achieve goals. "I can" statements: write a report stating that you can achieve your goals. For example, if you want to make an appointment with a new person, it is a good idea to say, "I can make an appointment with a new person." Several experts recommend avoiding any negative connotations. I will do: write a declaration stating that today you will use your skills to achieve your goal. So, following the example above, you can say, "I'm going out with someone new. Once again, the claim must use positive language and should clearly state what we are going to do today to reach the " lens long-term exposure match safer: feed some positive qualities with your goals. Which of the positive characters will help you achieve your goals? For example, if trying to talk to new people, you need courage or bravery.

You will need to show their repetition so that you can use them repetition is the key to ensuring the effectiveness of the affirmation you want to consider your statements several times a day every day Continue to use your affirmations the more something confirm, the more assertive you will mind accept it. If you are trying to achieve a short-term goal, use your statements until you reach r added. You want to use the claim as a counterattack. The script, practice each of them.

Examples of affirmations

To make your work easier, here is a list of examples of positive affirmations that work and which you can use to start with:

☐ I believe in my skills and abilities;

☐ My mistakes are seen as opportunities for development and learning;

☐ I'm still trying to grow to get better;

☐ I have power over my emotions; they don't control me;

☐ I am a brave leader;

☐ I attract love because I am myself, and people love it.

☐ They are an inexhaustible source of performance.

☐ I believe so deeply in myself.

☐ I achieve everything my soul adapts to.

☐ I fight negative and motivating thoughts.

☐ Trust is natural to me.

☐ And I grow up every day, and I have the power to change.

☐ I have strong faith in myself and my ability to succeed.

☐ My mind is open to all possibilities that surround me.

☐ I focus on my future and move forward in my life.

☐ My history does not determine who I am today.

☐ I trust my wisdom and intuition.

☐ I am the only person who knows what is best for me.

☐ My voice is important, and I will speak whenever I want.

☐ People listen to me because my words are precious.

Each of these statements will help you regain self-esteem in any situation or field. Self-confidence is a daily journey. And in this way, individual words, like sentences, have their meanings so that they cannot be underestimated.

# Chapter 18: How to set up and achieve all your goals

No one is born, knowing accurately how to set goals and how to make what they want in life. As with other things, goal setting is an art to learn and improve. Achieving goals is a crucial part of boosting confidence: it helps you model and updates precisely as it is defined while helping to increase your sense of accomplishment. Besides, setting goals will give you long-term vision and short-term motivation. More specifically, setting goals is a fundamental method:

☐ Deciding what you want to achieve in life.

☐ Separate what is essential and irrelevant.

☐ Motivate yourself.

☐ Develop your self-esteem based on your success in achieving your goals.

A useful way to strengthen your goals and increase your performance is to use the SMART method.

SMART means

S - Specific

M- Measurable

A- Achievable

R- Relevant

T -Time limit (or identifiable).

The SMART method was developed by Peter Drucker in 1954. It is a system used to identify, define, and search for specific and measurable goals. Let's see how it works and analyze each point in detail.

How to use the SMART approach to achieve goals

1.Specific

Your specific purpose must be clear and precise; otherwise, you cannot concentrate your efforts or feel motivated to achieve this goal. When writing your goal, try to answer the following questions:

o    What do I want to make?

o    Why is this goal important?

o    Who is involved?

o    Where is?

o    What resources or restrictions are included?

The more precisely it describes what you want to achieve, the more likely you can make it.


2.Measurable

It is essential to have measurable goals so that you can track your progress and stay motivated. Assessing your progress helps you stay focused, meet deadlines, and feel the emotions of achieving your goal. A measurable goal should answer questions such as:

o    How much it costs?

o    How much?

o    How do I know when it will be reached?

## 3.Achievable

Your goal must also be realistic and achievable to succeed. In other words, this should increase your skills, but still, be possible. By setting an attainable goal, you can identify previously ignored opportunities or resources that may bring you closer to it. The attainable goal generally answers questions like:

o     How can I achieve this goal?

o     How realistic is the goal based on other constraints such as financial factors?

This does not mean that you have to choose goals that are too small, easy to achieve, or irrelevant: the best solution is inside. You must set goals large enough to stimulate and motivate you to improve, but small enough to be possible and achievable.

## 4. Relevant

This step is to ensure that your goal is important to you and that it is in line with pertinent other purposes. We all need support and help to achieve our goals, but it's crucial to maintain control over them. So make sure your plans push everyone forward, but you're still responsible for achieving your goal. A suitable goal can answer "yes" to these questions:

- does this seem useful?

- Is this the right time?

- Does this suit our other efforts/needs?

- Am I the right person to achieve this?

- Does this apply in the current socio-economic context?

5.Time-bound

Every goal needs an actual date so that it has a period to focus on and something to work on. This part of the SMART goal criteria helps to prevent the priority of daily activities over their long-term goals. A time-limited target typically answers the following questions:

o    When?

o    What can I do in six months?

o    What can I do in six weeks?

o    What can I do today?

Along the way, there will be obstacles to overcome and unexpected events that can waste time, remember when you associate a date with a goal. Finally, remember the most essential thing: celebrate when you reach the goal before the deadline.

## Examples of SMART goals

Now that you know what a reasonable goal is, we'll look at some cases of successful joint planning using SMART goals.

As you can see, the objectives on the left are very vague, general, expired, and impossible to measure. On the other hand, the goals on the right are much more precise, motivating, and achievable. In short, .push you to the action! And this is the primary function of the goal.

## Other basic tips

In addition to the SMART approach, if you want to achieve your goals, you must also follow three essential tips:

1.Scrivili

Saving goals guarantees that you will think about every little detail and how each action will be updated to reach the goal. It also lets you remember goals because research has shown a strong correlation between writing and retaining memory.

2. Achieve your goals

Regularly It is crucial to track your goals weekly or monthly. See where you come from and see the small winnings you needed when traveling. Don't take these small successes for granted, and don't let them go unnoticed.

Whenever you achieve one of these goals, your brain will be conditioned to focus on what matters most and start making more!

## 3. Display

Another important tip is that you imagine that you have made your goals. Studies have shown that the motor parts of the brain will be activated during physical exercise. One study had two groups; one who practiced the piano physically and the others who played the piano mentally. Most interestingly, those who exercised through visualization were as effective as those who used physical. This means that you don't have to apply physically to be good at something. This study explains the power of visualization, and you should also use the display to improve any skills or achieve any goal.

## 4. Keep dilatation on targets

We have resistance many times and change when we need it most. Some discipline is required, but the benefits of quitting smoking to postpone are huge. Putting things away makes them harder and scary. There is nothing worse and more complicated than surviving unfinished business. It's like an extra weight on your arm that doesn't let you enjoy what you do. It just causes stress. Most of the time, you realize that the things you put off can be achieved very quickly, with the advantage that you will later feel much lighter and forget about it. Procrastination avoids something that needs to be done. He sets it aside in the hope that they will improve without doing anything about it. The problem is that most of the time, things don't educate themselves; They get worse Many times, the cause of delay is fear. Another source seems overwhelmed. You are delayed when

• do nothing instead of what you should do.

• Do something less important than what you should do.

• Do something more sensible than what we are supposed to do.


The key to start is simply this. Start. Usually, after running, you create enough dynamics to continue. Focus on the first step. And then another one. And one more thing: these small steps add results quite quickly. The only difference between people who achieve their goals and those who do not, between success and those who are not, is one thing: act. During the year, you will be grateful to start now. The only difference between what you want to be and what you are now is what you do from now on. Your actions will take you there. It will not be easy; it will be a pain, you will need willpower, sacrifice, patience, and you will have to make difficult decisions. It may also be necessary to let some people leave. It will be easier to get out many times. You'll want to give up a few times, but remember one thing: when you reach your goal, the whole victim will be worth it. "Is it worth bombing and losing sleep because of the work you could do in a few hours?" The best time to start any effort is always NOW! By collecting all these tips, you can plan and achieve your goals, thereby increasing your confidence.

## Chapter 19: Exercises to get out of the comfort zone

When you lack confidence, all you don't know or don't know what you can do is something that becomes painfully difficult to prove. When you try to do something new, you are worried about whether you will succeed, and this is scary. When he can't do what he does, he is ashamed and loses confidence. That's what you're trying to avoid by staying firmly in your comfort zone. However, when it stays in the comfort zone, it doesn't grow. Nobody and nothing grows thanks to comfort. Growing up is physically painful and requires effort, and just as body height or pregnancy can cause discomfort most of the time, mental and confidence increase will also cause some pain.

## Discomfort and confidence

When he feels uncomfortable, he is forced to find a way to change it. You may have no other choice but to act in a way that will not make you feel uncomfortable, for example, by trying to avoid the situation altogether, or you will have to solve a problem that worries you. This means that the options available are action or inaction, and if you choose no response, it will ensure that discomfort continues. However, when you select the work, you have the opportunity to end this discomfort. Of course, success is not guaranteed, but if you can act in some way, you can be sure that you have the chance to improve your situation. This means that you work in a way that is not a guarantee. This means that you can't be sure that what you are doing will be useful or if it turns out to be unsuccessful. Failure can make life difficult, but you can progress if you can. Success in the face of discomfort when he was afraid of failure when he acted for the first time means he can count on himself a bit more. You will be able to recognize that something you have done has worked, and that means you deserve a little more confidence than you were recently given. Therefore, if you want to grow, you need to make sure that you can leave the comfort zone.

Why leave the comfort zone

When you deliberately stay in the comfort zone, you risk something that can be even worse than failure: you risk complacency. Satisfaction is associated with inaction and refusal to do something beneficial to you. When you refuse to do something useful, you can't grow effectively. Such complacency can make you feel that everything goes as it is. However, if you are reading this book at the moment, you are probably not particularly happy with your life situation. You probably want to grow further because you know that you lack confidence and want to develop it further. But how do you learn to trust yourself and your skills if you never get the chance? Refusing to take this risk means you are effectively paralyzing. You are not trying to do something new. You will not learn new methods of dealing with the world around you.

You are not trying to make sure that you can make progress that you would like to see in yourself. Instead, it allows its potential waste without using them. You are not learning anything new. You are not doing anything new. Stay where you can't accept anything new. Remember, however, that trust does not come overnight. Trust that you build it, does not appear merely effortless. You need to give yourself space for development, which is associated with risks and sporadic learning failures.

Do something that scares you every day

When it's time to leave the comfort zone, you may not know where to start. After all, it's scary to change what you do or the way you do it. It may be easier if you ignore the change you are asking for to recognize it while remaining content. After all, failure can be too much for you: you prefer to be exactly where you are. However, this is the wrong mentality. You must be willing to leave this comfort zone, and the only way to accept that you will have to do it sometimes is to do it regularly. You want to know the discomfort, to stop seeing it as something to fear, and instead see it as a valuable resource: you want to be able to accept this discomfort as a motivation for change and development. Growing up is not easy. He comes with anxiety. If you are afraid of this discomfort, it will never happen. Therefore, the best way to learn about pain is to force yourself regularly. Think about how, entering a cold pool, every inch where you lower your foot into the water seems unbearable. It takes forever to get used to the cold, and you can give up before you have much more than one foot or leg. However, when you jump directly, the worst ends in a few seconds, and then you start to acclimatize. You and your body are much more able to handle the discomfort in what you believe, and you can jump alone. However, instead of jumping into the pool, you do one thing that scares you. It doesn't have to be scary: no one asks you for a parachute, so take a snake and then grab and hold the tarantula and do anything else that is a manifestation of your nightmares. However, you should do something that makes you feel mild or moderate discomfort once a day. Maybe it's an awkward conversation that you avoided. Perhaps he'll do a comedy while standing at a local bar, even though he has a crippling social phobia and isn't particularly funny. No matter what you choose, make sure there is one thing every day. In time, you will discover that you are developing tremendously, and you will love the person you become. Over time, you will trust yourself more and more. You will prove that unpleasant feelings are not the end of the world and that you can deal with them. You would allow yourself to deepen this discomfort so much that it is no longer hurting when you experience pain in real life. If someone compares you with a store, you will not be afraid that your order was placed incorrectly or that you did not receive the ordered product. Discomfort will still be present, but navigation is much easier than otherwise. This is extremely valuable: when you can quickly discover this discomfort in this way, you'll find that your development opportunities are almost limitless.

Break your routine

Sometimes complacency comes in the form of a rigorous routine that you follow day by day. This can be great for staying on track and making sure you always take care of everything you need to do, but not leaving this routine can lead to problems. It may become too stiff and depend on the specific program you are using. This means that dealing with any change in your routine may seem much worse than simply because you feel threatened by the idea of getting rid of it.

For this reason, sometimes it is better to run this procedure and do something else for a day or two. You will learn to fly through the seat of the pants, and you may feel anxious or afraid of trying to adjust everything in the new order, but that's fine! By eliminating your schedule for a day or two, you learn flexibility. Plans do not always agree, so sometimes, you should be flexible to your expectations, and the best way to do this is to learn to follow the trend when necessary. When you do this, you should consider your programs that exist for some reason. For example, if you need a schedule to make sure you get to class and work on time, maybe choosing a weekend to get rid of it will be best for you. However, we recommend that you try this from time to time. You will learn to cope with these changes better than ever, and there is a strength to be flexible in this way.

Try something new spontaneously

It doesn't necessarily have to be scary, or it doesn't necessarily make you feel uncomfortable, but sometimes spontaneous trying something new can be a fantastic way to get out of this comfort zone into the unknown. Again, he wants to make sure he's not afraid of the unknown, so what's a better way to try something new spontaneously? Perhaps your way to try something new is to go to a new place you don't know and decide to spend the day there without studying or planning. You can take a friend or someone with you to have this business, or you can do it all by yourself. No matter how you do it, you'll find that spending a day in an unknown place without floors is a great way to get out of the comfort zone.

What's more, try to ask people around you what they think you should do. Ask for advice on where to go for lunch or dinner, what is the fun in the area, and then follow the directions provided. When you do this, you'll find that you have to adapt to discomfort. You will quickly forget how uncomfortable you are and start having fun. This is an ideal lesson to learn to accept what surrounds you and throw yourself at everything that happens to you. Ultimately, the most essential thing in this exercise will be to make sure you can go and make sure you do what you should do in the face of the unknown and associated discomfort. By learning how to feel good with the unknown, you will find that you can think better and function in an emergency, simply because you have been forced to get used to this stress, and the benefit is convinced that you can trust yourself and your judgment more the more you can get out of the negativity that you find yourself in.

Chapter 20: Self-pity exercises

We are often willing to show compassion to everyone and everyone but us. We are ready for compassion for the people around us, but when it comes to compassion for ourselves, we tend to fight. It is much more difficult to look at yourself and say that you have made an honest mistake that you should not blame yourself than to tell an accidental stranger, especially when what happened was, in fact, an accidental honest error that was wholly involuntary and not too harmful. We tend to maintain higher standards than other people. Most of the time, we can justify it by saying that we know what we can do better than anyone else, so when we do not meet these expectations, we are prone to anger or anger. This leads to all types of negative spiral language. You can tell yourself that you were too stupid to do this job properly, and now there is a lot of clutter to fix. It can be said that the result of his great catastrophe is that he must help several people to make sure that they do not suffer from what went wrong. Compassion would, however, help ease this kind of negativity. When you feel sorry for yourself, you are much more likely to see things as they are and accept what happened. He is not going to hurt other people intentionally, but he is ready to take responsibility, too responsible. Of course, this leads to a breakdown of self-esteem. After all, if you tell yourself that you are unable, you must be unable.

Because compassion is important

Compassion is essential for a fundamental reason: when you sympathize with other people, you help them. People are social animals: we try to live in groups, and thus the ability to communicate with each other. Compassion is one way to communicate. When they are compassionate, they tell the other person that they care and want to help them at all costs. Your compassion shows that you do not get angry or angry because of what happened and that you are ready to help sort out the clutter in every possible way. When you feel for other people, you actively build relationships with them, developing a link that will lead you far in life. You need this relationship, so when you inevitably make a mistake, you will be treated with the same compassion.

## Compassion and self-esteem

However, some people don't think they deserve kindness. They can sympathize to help other people who fight in the same situation they find themselves in, but will not forgive themselves. They see their failure as an unforgivable flaw, and instead of trying to do something better in the future, they blame themselves in attempting to convey this message: errors are unacceptable. However, they are unacceptable only if they are yours. You will tolerate and help others with compassion when you find out that they have made a mistake, but you are not willing to give yourself the same forgiveness and kindness, all because you feel that you do not deserve it. This is problematic: when you treat yourself this way, you are saying that you don't care. You say that you must not make mistakes and that every mistake you make is unforgivable.

Think about the damage your self-esteem would do to you. If you can't make one mistake without deserving hatred or any violent reaction, what happens if you make a mistake? Sometimes we all make mistakes: you can't expect perfection from yourself when there is no perfection. However, you do it anyway and deny yourself forgiveness when you inevitably fail. This leads to a lack of self-esteem. Your self-esteem deteriorates over time until you feel so frustrated and disappointed in yourself that you can't be worse. By default, you see yourself as a problematic person, which leads to hatred. Self-hatred leads to low self-esteem. His low self-esteem leads him to fight for survival with the people around him, feeling that he is unable to do anything, and therefore the low self-esteem cycle continues.

## Develop compassion

Of course, there is a way: you can learn to feel sorry for yourself. When you are ready to forgive yourself mistakes, you'll find that you are not afraid to make these mistakes first. The ability to forgive yourself and compassion is one of the best things you can do for yourself. After all, you are the person closest to you. Spend your whole life with you, and yet you are incredibly quick to criticize yourself every time you feel you have made a mistake. If someone told you about how you talk to yourself, would you listen? Do you want to stay in this relationship? Would you be willing to leave instead of being criticized continuously and feel that you are not worth any love or attachment? You probably don't have such a relationship. If you can't tolerate someone who treats you that way, why would you tolerate him? After all, you are the only person who should be treated better than any other person and considered himself absolute rubbish. This is an excellent warning sign and one of the main reasons why you should work on yourself. Work in your life means that you are ready to forgive yourself and treat yourself kindly as you deserve. The rest of this chapter will focus on giving you three ways to feel sorry for yourself, to help yourself be kind to yourself once and for all. When you are kind to yourself, your self-esteem will improve. When you upgrade your self-esteem, you'll find that you enjoy life much more and don't cope with your failures at the end of the world.

Forgive yourself regularly

When you're generally offended with yourself and your behavior towards other people, one of the best things you can do is to forgive yourself usually actively. When you are ready to forgive yourself regularly, you can free yourself of this pain and start treatment once and for all. When you are angry, it usually hurts. After all, your anger and resentment are symptoms of another problem, and if you find out what the problem is, you'll find that you can begin to solve it. However, it will be difficult for you to determine what the problem is if you are too angry to think about it. Therefore, he must be willing to forgive himself; Sometimes, it's easier to breathe deeply and forgive yourself than to get angry at what happened. After all, what has been done and cannot be changed. This means that you have no choice but to move on regardless of the result. When you forgive yourself, make sure you do it completely and thoroughly. Remember to tell yourself that you recognize that you are suffering and that you want everything to improve. Remember that everything will be fine, and what has happened does not mean that you are a terrible person or you are unable. Tell yourself that you forgive yourself and understand it. Stop feeling resentful and start focusing on your progress. In this way, you will find that you are happier.

Focus on growth

Another way to start feeling sorry for yourself is to focus on how you can grow instead of watching how you are held back. When you look at a situation and begin to discover what you can learn from it instead of what damage has occurred, you can recognize that it wasn't as bad as it seemed. You want to be able to realize that you can learn from this error. When you stop focusing on the unfortunate result that happened and focus on what you have learned, it turns out that this part of anger has dissipated. Imagine, for example, that you said something terrible that hurt your spouse. You know your spouse is angry, and you feel awful about it. Instead of solving the problem, however, you get depressed and stop at what you are saying. This is not particularly advantageous: you will not see any benefit in this. It's not helpful for you or your partner, and you suffer without knowing what to do. But instead of sitting and experiencing, what would happen if you concentrated on what you did wrong? You can learn from it, and by recognizing what you have learned, you can alleviate some of this pain. For example, remember that you can always improve in the future, and that's why I sincerely apologize to your partner. In doing so, he explains that he wants to move forward and that he legally apologizes for what happened.

## Develop awareness

The ultimate solution that will allow you to move forward and show your compassion is to learn to use consciousness. When you learn to practice mindfulness, you will enable yourself to learn to control your emotions. You learn that you don't have to experience all these negative feelings that hurt you; you can afford to move away from these emotions, and by leaving, you can start to heal. He is compassionate: you are actively giving yourself the distance you need to improve. When you want to develop awareness, you are learning how to come up with a method that you can use to focus your mind. You learn the best way to group and then deal with a given situation. You will learn to deal with all these destructive emotions that may have been problematic. While you can, you can heal. When you improve, you can learn. Perhaps the best and easiest way to use awareness is an awareness meditation. You learn that you are merely present in your current mental state without judgment or interference. You only need one point to observe the feelings you need to understand your mental state better. It also helps you start experiencing emotions without reacting to them. This means that you can help eliminate negative feelings and self-tampering. You may feel angry, not allowing yourself to look down. Then you can continue in peace without feeling that you have to hate yourself longer. To meditate on awareness, start by finding a quiet place to focus. You don't need much time, at the beginning you only need a few minutes. Start by taking a deep breath. Try to pull it out for four or five seconds during inhalation, feeling the air dilate your lungs. Then hold it for a few seconds and let it out slowly through your mouth. Repeat this process several times until you feel relaxed. When you do this, focus only on the air you breathe. Allow yourself to focus on this feeling of breathing when you allow your mind to try anything. When you do this, try to focus your thoughts on these breaths. If you notice that your account is wandering, try to ignore it and concentrate again. The purpose of this is to make sure that you distance yourself from bad feelings, focus on breathing, and allowing yourself to see how you feel. When you're done, you'll find that you feel much calmer:

you can focus more easily on your thoughts and less actively sabotage.

Chapter 21: Sharpen your passions to build self-esteem

Now that you have a clear idea of your hidden potentials, I need you to stay away and let yourself feel good with them. This shows clearly that it is not useless, and even more so, it is not. You have the potential to be an individual person. You have raw ingredients. Is there; It's just below the surface.

In many cases, you don't want it to happen, but it is. You must recognize the list of your hidden and visible potential. Now look at this list and let yourself feel good. Let me state that you are not entirely useless, that there is nothing wrong with you, and that nothing is missing. You have the raw materials to succeed. Of course, transforming potential into reality requires work. Attention to detail, perseverance, and consistency are necessary. Still, it's a great victory for you when you recognize that you have all these things for yourself. There is no need for false modesty.

You don't have to sabotage a positive feeling, saying, "Well, everyone has potential." or "They're just one face in the crowd because everyone has the potential not to grow." Forget about it. Focus only on the fact that you have this potential, and you have the opportunity to develop it so that you can make the most of your prospects. You have it inside It shows in white that you have ingredients by size, you have to connect the points; You need to mix the ingredients. In other words, you must act according to what you already have. It's not like I'm proactively getting something I don't currently have. It's already there. I want you to focus on it and make you feel good. This is something to celebrate; There is something to be happy with. It's part of who you are and what you have to offer to the universe. The next step is to look at these raw ingredients and build them.

Take your passions and build them

Develop yourself and develop your passions. If you are passionate about specific activities, do them in any way. The more you do something that gives you satisfaction and happiness, the more you invest in your personal goal. The more often you do it, the more you invest in your self-esteem. How it works is very simple. The more you develop your passions, the more competent you will be. They are no longer just potential; This is no longer just a theoretical set of functions that is worth developing. When you work on it, sharpen and build, it affects your reality because you can see its impact. For example, if you like to sing in the shower, you can continue your passion for singing. You can start getting out of the shower, take singing lessons, and then risk opening the evening with a microphone at your local club, bar, or lounge. Now everyone can sing, so you don't have to feel out of place. However, when you get there, meet the crowd and discover your soul, it is a huge victory. Why don't you do it for them; You do it for yourself. You do it to follow the process.

You came from someone who hides this huge personal light under the singing bowl in the shower, to someone who dared to sing in front of the audience. This victory, no matter what happens later, is essential for you to make this journey. This is a huge transition. Celebrate when you develop your passions. This is extremely important because the more you celebrate, the more you sink. However, there is nothing wrong with you. It's worth respecting, it's worth loving, and it's worth something. The more you accept yourself, the more your self-esteem will increase. The secret is to be aware of the process. This is key; Not only are you enjoying the journey. Don't get me wrong, there are many values. But that has a purpose; You should also pay attention to the character you are building. You know you do it for a reason; You do it because you have low self-esteem and want to develop and transform it so that you can project yourself to ever-higher levels of confidence. This is very difficult unless you focus the laser on the transition from a shy and suffering from a sense of inadequacy and low self-esteem to a person who believes that he can actively change his reality. In other words, someone who works from a place of extraordinary confidence.

## Self-esteem is based on the success

Now many people may think that this is terrible news. After all, we live in a modern society where confidence should be a reward at the door. If you've been to a public school in the United States, you know exactly what I'm talking about. Most school curricula emphasize self-confidence rather than ensuring that children follow a traditional curriculum to achieve academic excellence. The old standard was indeed right. Confidence comes later; it is a precursor of faith. It's like building a massive tower. You can't make a tower in the sand; It will sink. You will fall over and kill people in the tower. I mean, it's common sense.

Similarly, you can't build confidence without foundation. How will you build your self-esteem? And that's why you must first focus on your passions, interests, discover more, and then make the transition to feel good with your potential, challenge your potential, celebrate your potential and celebrate your confidence. In other words, you must first do something about your passions. Objectivity appears here. As I said before, the world does not care about your feelings; the only thing that matters is what you do or what you do. By playing with his passions, grinding, and participating, he begins to make something happen. You start to improve your interests. Again, taking the example of singing, singing in the shower is one thing, and the puppy's voice is tortured to death. It's great to know your inner passions. It's fantastic that you sang and discovered that you must find your soul. However, you can't leave it there. You need to refine your passion. You must be good at it. If your voice sounds like a tortured puppy to death, you need to keep working on your love until it looks good. See how it works This is where the result appears; This is where the real world intervenes. It's easy to feel good about subjective things like oh, and you have to contact your passion and undress your soul, entertaining your love. Behind closed doors is fine, but ultimately it must have external verification. In other words, you must be kind enough to say that I have achieved something objectively. I took something that interested me, and I was passionate about it, and I worked so much that others would agree that I'm good at it. In other words, I have achieved it. This is crucial because otherwise, all these advances would be just subjective. It would be simply selfish and private. This will not move the needle to the point where self-esteem appears. True self-confidence is based on success. When you become good at something, you allow yourself to feel good and say to yourself, "I am good at something. I'm good at it. " By doing this, he creates his personal space; It's a space that nobody can take from you because you worked on it. See how it works Self-esteem is based on success. It is not a priori that someone falls on you because you have appeared. This is not a prize at the door; It's built on something substantial. In other words, you worked on it, and it makes it real. You need to continue working on your passions; You must be useful to them. I know it will be a bit delicate. I know it will hurt many people who read it, but I have to say it. You must allow yourself, after a while, criticism. You must submit to an objective standard. Before this point, everything is subjective, and everything concerns your feelings. How well you feel, how justified you are, how honored you feel, It is perfect, but as soon as your passion takes over and gives up the external evaluation, then you know when it achieved. Otherwise, it's okay. This is where the trait of immunity appears.

Hit an obstacle on the road and fail; ok. You have to go back, continue working, try again until you can. Be open to corrections and corrections. Don't be afraid of judgment; Don't be scared of criticism. Cure; strives to be the best in what you are passionate about. Use your passion as fuel to do everything you need or until you recover. Let's face it, when you work on something, there are many days when you don't want to try it. There are many days when you just want to give up. This is where honest passion begins. Because if you're passionate about it, you'll take advantage of this internal energy and get the power you need to keep pushing.

Building on objective foundations of excellence

When you become perfect at something, you will feel more confident. It has a solid and objective basis for self-esteem, which is good at something. It's not just an illusion; You are not just hypnotizing or deceiving yourself. This is true because it can be traced back to real results. Compare this to the appearance in school and that everyone gets the letter A or participates in a sport, and no one loses because everyone gets a medal. The sense of fulfillment in this context is destroyed. There is nothing to work on because if you try to sacrifice or loosen, the result will be the same. This is not how the real world works. The real world gives you the right to feel good because you have something objective to feel good about. In other words, it rests on solid foundations of success.

## You are only useful as the last victory

Now, if you think the previous section is a little confusing, I have bad news for you, it's a little worse. The truth is you are as good as your last win. When was the last time you met people who remember the old days? They told you, "Oh yes, I made a million dollars five months ago," or "Ten years ago, I traveled the world." Although such claims may be excellent in terms of sharing shared memories, sooner or later, they become old and outdated. They can be very annoying. You see, the world is focused not only on the results it produces but also on the present. In other words, can you get good results now? While gravity and the tremendous value of what you have done in the past have some effect, the more distant the result, the less the world will be. He has a short-term memory, whether he likes it or not. That's why you should understand that when it comes to getting results, you are as good as your last win. Do not rest on your laurels. Allow yourself to be involved continuously, continually improve your skills, always challenge yourself. This results in continuous improvement; You are always looking for the next biggest and best action when it comes to your passions. This gives you a substantial competitive advantage over people trying to do what you do. They can't hold a candle if you're passionate because you're continually improving. The difference is like black and white because you invest in continuous improvement.

## Climb the spiral stairs towards higher self-esteem

Believe it or not, continuous improvement of your passion leads to increased self-esteem. Start with your desires. Therefore, he improves them to get better results. You get objective verification. People would say, "Wow! Do you sing better now than before? ", You earn more money now than before "or" You live in a larger house now than before "or" You are "more respected now than before."

In any case, and regardless of your passion, objective validation increases. So it increases your self-esteem because you say clearly: "I'm doing something right. I took my passions, improved myself, and can objectively demonstrate that I have reached a higher level. When you feel taller, your level of passion increases, your "gas tank" of passion is full and has more energy to go to the next level of improved performance, objective verification, etc. It is a spiral upwards of increasing self-esteem. With each increase, it is also a more massive projection, which means that there is an external manifestation; their self-esteem is more visible. People who are good at what they do are becoming more and more confident, and the harder they are to hide and explain. They become optimistic, the more they succeed because the world sits and draws attention. See how the upward spiral works?

## Proposal

Congratulations! You have reached the end of the book "Self-confidence and self-esteem."

When you get here, you must recognize that you have done something from beginning to end, and you deserve to acknowledge this result for yourself. You may have stopped reading, but you decided not to accept and accept my most enormous gratitude. Reading this book, I hope that it will prove useful and informative. I hope you feel a little better prepared to solve your problems with confidence once and for all.

In summary, remember that in this book, you discussed how your self-esteem affects almost every aspect of your life, and vice versa, your own life also directly affects your self-esteem. This means that you need to perform a careful balancing act: you must be able to gently balance this line to make sure that not everything collapses with self-esteem.

From now on, options for further action are numerous. You can choose to implement the behaviors and activities described in this book. You can learn to use these many tools to fully utilize your potential to unlock your confidence once and for all. You can decide that you need therapy instead, and this is another good option to do here. You can study self-esteem, a closely related topic that has already been discussed in connection with this book. You can consider cognitive-behavioral therapy or other forms of cognitive restructuring to help you deal with negative thoughts. Ultimately, what you choose will be the right choice for you.

However, as you progress, remember that it is worth more than you think. Although you may look negative and doubt who you are as a person, remember that there are people around you who love you and count on you. These people need you, and they enjoy life. No matter how bad you feel, remember that you add value to this world, and you must recognize it. No matter how little confidence you have, you should remember that what you have is necessary to protect and strengthen it. Over time, you'll find that you like who you are. You can reach the point where you look in the mirror, and you want the reflection you see. You can do it, however difficult it may seem at first. All you have to do is make an effort and succeed.

Finally, thank you for reading this book and letting me keep my hand on the road to a healthy level of confidence. If you have found that this book has provided you with some benefit by helping you see what you need to improve or find out exactly how you see yourself and what you will do next, you can leave a comment on Amazon. Your feedback and comments will always be appreciated and encouraged. Yet again, thank you and good luck on the journey to find self-confidence and self-esteem.


Thank You

CPSIA information can be obtained
at www.ICGtesting.com
Printed in the USA
BVHW041512190321
602997BV00010B/450